100
GREATS

MIDDLESEX
COUNTY CRICKET CLUB

'Mr Middlesex' Pelham Warner, as seen by RIP.

100 GREATS

MIDDLESEX
COUNTY CRICKET CLUB

COMPILED BY
ROBERT BROOKE

TEMPUS

Key:
The letters at the top of the page refer to the following batting or bowling styles:

RHB – right-handed batsman
LHB – left-handed batsman
OB – off-break bowler
LBG – right-armed bowler of leg breaks and googlies
SLA – slow left-arm spin
RFM – right-arm fast medium pace
RF – right-arm fast pace
LF – left-arm fast pace
LM – left-arm medium pace
LFM – left-arm fast medium pace
RM – right-arm medium pace
LB – leg break bowler
WK – wicketkeeper

First published 2003

Tempus Publishing Limited
The Mill, Brimscombe Port,
Stroud, Gloucestershire, GL5 2QG

© Robert Brooke, 2003

The right of Robert Brooke to be identified as the Author
of this work has been asserted in accordance with the
Copyrights, Designs and Patents Act 1988.

British Library Cataloguing in Publication Data.
A catalogue record for this book is available from the British Library.

ISBN 0 7524 2746 6

Typesetting and origination by Tempus Publishing Limited
Printed in Great Britain by Midway Colour Print, Wiltshire

Preface

When I was asked by James Howarth of Tempus to compile this work containing short essays and statistical details of 100 Middlesex Cricketers, it was emphasised that it would be a personal choice.

I therefore feel I owe readers an explanation as to why, for instance, so few of Middlesex's recent high-performing overseas players were included. The simple reason is that this is a book about Middlesex cricket and cricketers and I do not feel that such high performers as, for instance, Vincent van der Bijl were genuine Middlesex cricketers in the strictest sense of the term. There are, however, exceptions. Wayne Daniel, for instance, I feel sure came to regard himself as a Middlesex cricketer above all else and I regarded him as an automatic choice. Then there is Desmond Haynes, who I felt played just long enough to justify inclusion, but it was a close thing.

With regard to my top twenty, I feel there will be little argument in nineteen of the cases. As for Harry Sharp, this epitome of the old-fashioned London professional cricketer, and one of my cricket heroes, I offer no apologies for including him, and to dedicating this book to him.

Finally, my best team. Again, a personal choice, but I feel this team would take some beating, with each player at his peak:

Jack Robertson
Frank Tarrant
Pat Hendren
Mike Gatting
Denis Compton
Jack W Hearne
Walter Robins (capt)
Albert Trott
John Murray
Jack T Hearne
Alan Moss

Some of those I have omitted!

Acknowledgements

James Howarth, Ruth Potter and Kate Wiseman of Tempus, Roger Wootton for the cover photograph and other photographs, Roger Mann, Phil Britt, David Kendix and Peter Wynne-Thomas. Mike Gatting OBE, for the favour of a foreword, Brian Heald and the late Derek Lodge, compilers of the official *Middlesex Records Book*, J.W. Hearne junior, David Goodyear, for photographic help, and Arthur Wentworth.

The three Studd brothers in 1906 – J.E.K. Studd (left),
C.T. Studd (middle), G.B. Studd (right).

Foreword

All followers of Middlesex County Cricket Club will I'm sure join me in welcoming Robert Brooke's fine book of 100 great Middlesex cricketers. This provides an opportunity to reflect on the players who, over the club's long and distinguished history, have performed so well and delivered so much success.

Amongst the 100 names are plenty who were internationally renowned England players – the likes of 'Plum' Warner, Patsy Hendren, Denis Compton and Bill Edrich. Then, more recently, there were the overseas cricketers who did so much to revitalise the county game such as Wayne Daniel and Desmond Haynes. But there are also many players here whose distinguished service for the club may not be so readily remembered. They may never have played Test cricket, but their team contribution was just as vital as any star name. Take for example Harry Sharp, with nearly sixty years' service to Middlesex and MCC as player, coach, umpire and finally scorer.

Enjoy this book and look forward with me to the emergence from the Lord's pavillion of the next 100 great Middlesex cricketers in the years to come.

Mike Gatting OBE
Enfield, Middlesex
February 2003

100 Middlesex Greats

G.O.B. *Allen*
G.D. Barlow
P.I. Bedford
G.W. Beldam
D. Bennett
D.A. Bick
B.J.T. Bosanquet
J.M. Brearley
K.R. Brown
S.M. Brown
C.F. Buller
G. Burton
R.O. Butcher
J.D. Carr
E.A. Clark
D.C.S. Compton
L.H. Compton
N.G. Cowans
W.W Daniel
J.G. Dewes
J. Douglas
P.R. Downton
F.J. Durston
W.J. Edrich
P.H. Edmonds
J.E. Emburey
N.G. Featherstone
F.G.J. Ford
A.R.C. Fraser
R.A. Gale
M.W. Gatting
L.H. Gray
W.H. Hadow
N.E. Haig
G.E. Hart
H.B. Hayman
D.L. Haynes

J.T. Hearne
J.W. Hearne
T. Hearne
E.H. Hendren
P.J.T. Henery
R.W. Hooker
J.H.A. Hulme
E.T. Killick
A.H. Latchman
H.W. Lee
R.S. Lucas
A. Lyttelton
G. MacGregor
F.T. Mann
F.G. Mann
A.E. Moss
J.T. Murray
H.R. Murrell
Sir T.C. O'Brien
P.H. Parfitt
I.A.R. Peebles
J. Phillips
J.S.E. Price
W.F.F. Price
C.T. Radley
M.R. Ramprakash
J.T. Rawlin
J. Robertson
J.D.B. Robertson
R.W.V. Robins
M.A. Roseberry
W.E. Russell
S.W. Scott
M.W.W. Selvey
O.A. Shah
H.P.H. Sharp
J.M. Sims

W.N. Slack
C.I.J. Smith
M.J. Smith
G.T.S. Stevens
A.E. Stoddart
A.J. Strauss
C.T. Studd
G.B. Studd
F.A. Tarrant
A.W. Thompson
C.I. Thornton
F.J. Titmus
A.E. Trott
P.C.R. Tufnell
G.F. Vernon
I.D. Walker
R.D. Walker
V.E. Walker
Sir P.F. Warner
J.J. Warr
A.J. Webbe
P.N. Weekes
C.M. Wells
J.E. West
N.F. Williams
J.A. Young

The twenty who appear here in italics, occupy two pages instead of the usual one.

Sir George Oswald Browning Allen

RHB, RF, 1921-1950

Born: 31 July 1902, Bell View Hill, Sydney, Australia

Died: 29 November 1989, St John's Wood, London

Batting

M	I	NO	Runs	Av
146	210	28	4667	25.64
50	100	ct/st		
23	4	56		

Bowling

Balls	Runs	Wkts	Av	5wI	10wM
18671	8668	420	20.64	27	3

Best Performances
155 v Surrey at The Oval, 1929
10-40 v Lancashire at Lord's, 1929

'Gubby' Allen was a true amateur in that he only played first-class cricket when his work in the city so permitted. The effect of this was that he was never a regular Middlesex player and in fact he never scored 1,000 runs or took 100 wickets in any one season. Nonetheless Allen's was a statistically impressive career and he fully deserved his reputation as an outstanding all-rounder who won 25 caps for England.

Allen played 146 times for Middlesex over twenty-nine years. He was a valuable middle-order batsman whose basically sound technique enabled him to score runs in the top class into his late forties, despite the shortage of regular practice.

The highest of his 4 Middlesex centuries was 155 against Surrey at The Oval in 1929 and it was arguably his best. The innings lasted 200 minutes and was marked by sure driving after an uncertain start. Throughout his innings, which occupied the first afternoon and evening, Allen was in partnership with Harry Lee. They added 319 for the second wicket, a huge stand which put his side into a position to go for a win and yet at the time was only the third best for that particular wicket. Allen's final century for Middlesex

was 136 against Worcestershire at Lord's in 1936. It took 198 minutes and he added 211 for the sixth wicket with Joe Hulme. Two years earlier the same pair had put on 212 for the same wicket against Glamorgan at Lord's. Though his century-scoring was long over, as late as 1949 Allen shared in a stand of 230 for the fourth wicket with Jack Robertson against Worcestershire. There were four century stands in a total of 623-5 (all on the first day) and Gubby Allen was possibly disappointed at being bowled by Charlie Palmer for 98.

If Allen's batting relied mainly on a range of orthodox strokes his bowling was somewhat more explosive. His best feat – by a distance – was when he took all 10 in an innings for 40 runs against Lancashire at Lord's in 1929. Allen sent down 25.3 overs, 8 of the 10 victims were bowled and he had one run of 4 wickets in 5 balls. As interesting, perhaps, is the fact that both the other wickets came via wicketkeeper Fred Price, and one was stumped. Perhaps a minor point is that Middlesex never looked likely to win the match and were indeed fortunate to escape with a draw. Another fine performance by Allen was 8 for 58 (innings) and 13 for 148 (match) against Sussex at Hove in

'Gubby Allen' – a Gentleman at Scarborough.

1934. As with his all 10 the amount of support Allen received was strangely meagre and Middlesex were again lucky to scrape a draw.

'Gubby' Allen was a Cambridge Blue and captained England 11 times in 25 Tests.

It is surely something of a paradox that despite his playing career being so affected by business he was one of the busiest cricket administrators ever. From 1931 he was on the Middlesex committee and from 1933 to 1963 he was an MCC committeeman. He remained a powerful influence at Lord's almost until his death, being MCC president in 1963/64 and treasurer from 1964 to 1976. Allen was also an England selector from 1955 to 1961, and committee chairman each year.

Despite his pre-eminence 'Gubby' remained approachable and unassuming. Allen's home backed onto Lord's and it is said he had his personal entrance gate into the ground. He was appointed CBE in 1974 and in 1986 his services to cricket were recognised with a knighthood.

He was from a cricket family and his uncle R.C. Allen played for Australia against England in 1886/87 (and seemed to be one of those lucky people able to live comfortably without working). Despite his Australian background, however, 'Gubby' Allen, one of whose ancestors was a transported convict, was brought to England aged 6 and became completely Anglicised.

Graham Derek Barlow
LHB, RM, 1969-1986

Born: 26 March 1950, Folkestone, Kent

Batting

M	I	NO	Runs	Av
239	385	57	11640	35.48
244	229	21	5800	27.88

50	100	ct/st
54	23	131
32	5	87

Bowling

Balls	Runs	Wkts	Av	5wI	10wM
121	66	3	22.00	-	-
117	109	5	21.80	-	-

Best Performances
177 v Lancashire at Southport, 1981
158 v Lancashire at Lord's, 1984

Graham Barlow was a stylish and courageous left-handed batter, most at home and most effective in one of the opening positions, and a brilliant field in the covers. He was never able to transfer his county form into the Test arena, scoring only 17 runs for an average of 4.25, though it is arguable whether three Tests constitute a fair trial. For Middlesex, however, he was a valuable and popular team member whose enforced retirement in 1986 through back trouble was regarded as a big loss to the county.

Barlow first appeared for Middlesex in 1969 but did not immediately establish himself, waiting until 1976 before being capped. He eventually exceeded 1,000 runs for the county in seven seasons, with a best of 1,545 runs, average 48.28, in 1983. Barlow also established a good opening rapport with Wilf Slack and against Kent at Lord's in 1981 the pair were involved in an unbroken stand of 367. This was the Middlesex first wicket record at the time, and remains the best for that wicket at Lord's, and the best unbroken stand for any wicket for or against Middlesex. Barlow and

Slack also added 225 against Surrey at The Oval in 1985 and 203 against Leicestershire at Lord's in the same season. Barlow also distinguished himself against Northamptonshire at Lord's in 1983. He and Andy Miller exceeded 100 for the first wicket in each innings – yet finished on the losing side.

For his county Barlow scored 23 centuries, most of them watchful, but with the attractive style of the left hander, yet perhaps his most notable innings came when he carried his bat for 44 out of 83 against Essex on a Chelmsford 'greentop', with Derek Pringle in devastating form in 1983. Barlow also scored a second innings century as his side fought out a most unlikely draw.

In limited overs cricket Barlow enjoyed his days of success, most notably a marvellous, match-winning 158 against Lancashire at Lord's in the 1984 NatWest Trophy. Barlow scored many more than all the opposition batsmen combined.

Barlow, who obtained a degree at Lough-borough University was an all round sportsman who also played Rugby Union for Rosslyn Park.

Philip Ian Bedford

RHB, LBG, 1947-1962

Born: 11 February 1930, Friern Barnet
Died: 18 September 1966, Wanstead, Essex

Batting

M	I	NO	Runs	Av
65	64	18	722	15.69
50	100	ct/st		
2	-	34		

Bowling

Balls	Runs	Wkts	Av	5wI	10wM
6471	3370	103	32.71	4	-

Best Performances
75* v. Gloucestershire at Gloucester, 1961
6-52 v. Yorkshire at Bradford, 1951

Ian Bedford was every schoolboy's idol when, as an angelic-looking seventeen-year-old, just out of Woodhouse Grammar School, Finchley, he took 6 wickets for 135 on his first-class debut against Essex at Lord's in 1947, and a few days later took a further 6 against Notts. Weeks later was an innings analysis of 5-53 in 24.2 overs against Surrey at Lord's, his victims including Fishlock, Squires and Parker, and the following week in the last championship match of Middlesex's glad season, when all the applause was for Compton's equalling Hobbs' season century tally, he dismissed Lancashire's Washbrook, Place, Ikin, Wharton and Geoff Edrich, a top five of class and accomplishment, for 54 runs in 26 overs.

It was hoped that here was a new giant; certainly his bowling bordered on the genius rating. He had a high action and sharp spin, but his biggest asset was stated to be his subtle flight. The following months saw him grow and when cricket resumed the flight had gone. Bedford remained a good bowler, and rather better than his own rating of himself but those who had such high hopes of the schoolboy prodigy were to be disappointed. After

National Service, Bedford seemed happy with a business career and club cricket with Finchley, where his bowling remained valuable and his aggressive batting saw him approach all-rounder status.

Bedford was surprisingly brought back as captain in 1961 but after finishing third the county slumped in 1962 and Bedford seemed relieved to return to Finchley. He underused himself as a bowler but had one special day of glory with the bat. Going in with 91 needed for victory but 7 wickets down at Gloucester in 1961, Bedford made 75 not out in 40 minutes with 7 sixes, and adding 66 for the last wicket with Sturt he hit his side to a most unlikely 1 wicket victory. His last first-class appearance was for MCC in Dublin in September 1966. Twelve days later, batting for Finchley against Buckhurst Hill he collapsed at the wicket and died on the way to hospital. Thus the saddest of ends for a man apparently universally liked and respected. And, for a few short weeks in 1947 the seventeen-year-old schoolboy was one of the best spinners in England.

George William Beldam
RHB, RM, 1900-1907

Born: I May 1868, New Cross, Kent
Died: 23 November 1937, Lower Bourne,
  Farnham, Surrey

Batting

M	I	NO	Runs	Av
102	172	13	4796	30.16
50	100	ct/st		
21	7	66		

Bowling

Balls	Runs	Wkts	Av	5wI	10wM
4892	2063	76	27.14	3	-

Best Performances
155* v. Surrey at Lord's, 1902
5-28 v. Lancashire at Liverpool, 1902

George Beldam was a very steady batsman who began his Middlesex career late but was still perhaps a little unlucky not to have gone further than county cricket.

Beldam made an impressive start to his county career, scoring 62 on his debut in 1900 against Sussex at Lord's and adding 141 for the second wicket with Warner. Though playing fairly often it was not until 1902 that he made his maiden hundred, a superb unbeaten 155 in 270 minutes against Surrey at Lord's. Cecil Headlam helped him add 130 for the last wicket but abject performances from their batting colleagues led to a 10-wicket defeat. The following season saw Beldam score 89, 118 and 112 against Surrey with an attack including Richardson and Lockwood clearly holding no terrors for him. In 1904 he had his best season, scoring 917 runs, average 36.68, and the most notable of his three centuries was 140 against Somerset at Lord's when he was at the wickets 190 minutes and he added 201 for the fifth wicket with his cousin E.A. Beldam. Something of a decline set in after

1904 but he still remained a useful member of the side, when able to turn out. Beldam's slow bowling was also most useful at times. In 1902 he had figures of 5 for 28 in 10.1 overs against Lancashire and actually took all the second innings wickets to fall in a rain-ruined match. Perhaps he should have bowled more often.

Beldam turned out frequently for London County and MCC, and his full first-class figures were 6,562 runs (30.23) and 107 wickets.

Whatever his on-field exploits, George Beldam, whose family were originally Huguenot refugees and who was probably related to the old Hambledon cricketer, 'Silver Billy' Beldam, is more famous as the virtual inventor of action photography in cricket and other sports. Until he came along cricket photographs had been posed and somewhat 'wooden'. Beldam brought them to life. He was responsible for the photographs in a number of books and in 2000 a book, *Great Cricketers*, was published giving the story of Beldam and his life as photographer and cricketer, and artist, lavishly illustrated with examples of Beldam's work.

Donald Bennett

RHB, RMF, 1950-1968

Born: 18 December 1933, Wakefield, Yorkshire

Batting

M	I	NO	Runs	Av
392	590	120	10274	21.85
50	100	ct/st		
32	4	156		

Bowling

Balls	Runs	Wkts	Av	5wI	10wM
41477	19790	748	26.45	22	1

Best Performances
117* v. Kent at Maidstone, 1961
7-47 v. Sussex at Hove, 1956

When Yorkshire-born but Middlesex-reared Don Bennett made his first-class debut against Lancashire at Old Trafford in 1950 he was a mere 16 years and 200 days old and the third youngest to play for Middlesex. Bennett's performances on figures in his first season were unremarkable but he batted, bowled and, especially, fielded with great gusto and the county were hopeful of a bright future for the stocky teenager. Eighteen years and 392 matches later Bennett finally stepped out of first-class cricket; his services had been varied in the extreme and he had become one of only five Middlesex players to have exceeded 10,000 runs and 500 wickets in a county career. And yet he never really reached the very highest standards, as many expected him to do as a precocious teenager. Even his appearance in 1964 as the County's youngest ever beneficiary, seemed to slip by unnoticed. Possibly here was someone taken too much for granted, but certainly he was part of his side's backbone for a long time.

Don Bennett's best batting season was 1953 when unerring consistency brought the nine-teen-year-old 1,077 runs, average 28.34. He repeated the feat in 1955 – fewer runs and lower average – but never again. He was in fact rarely able to get in high enough to build a long innings, though on occasion he was involved in high late wicket stands. The best was an unbroken seventh-wicket stand of 220 with John Murray against Yorkshire at Leeds in 1964, and three years earlier he added 182 for the same wicket with the same player against Glamorgan. These stands remain the county's third and fourth best for this wicket. There should have been more of them. In bowling his best return was 78 wickets, average 22.08, in 1964 (interestingly he was given the new ball more frequently than usual). As an all-rounder he never did better than in 1956, with 904 runs (25.11) and 70 wickets (25.71). He was always showing that here was an all-rounder with a great deal of natural ability, yet for some reason, he was never to fulfill the best hopes.

After giving up as a player Bennett became county coach; it was a position for which he soon seemed admirably suited. He retired in 1997.

Donald Albert Bick
RHB, OB, 1954-1967

Born: 22 February 1936, Hampstead, Middlesex

Died: 24 January 1992, Ware, Hertfordshire

Batting

M	I	NO	Runs	Av
145	189	31	2136	13.51
50	100	ct/st		
8	-	35		

Bowling

Balls	Runs	Wkts	Av	5wI	10wM
15056	6328	229	27.63	5	-

Best Performances
67 v. Cambridge University at Fenner's, 1957
5-22 v. Yorkshire at Scarborough, 1959, and v. Cambridge University at Fenner's, 1965

It is surely being unfair to no one to suggest that Don Bick is the least distinguished cricketer featured in this book, and yet as a 'bread-and-butter' cricketer continually moved into the team, and out again, with no clearly defined role, but always giving of his best, he surely deserves his place. It seems he was perpetually 'young Don Bick' until suddenly he was in his thirties and finally released not too long after being capped.

It was possibly Bick's own uncertainty as to his place in the scheme of things which contributed to his inability to establish himself but there was surely little doubt as to his dedication. Bick made his debut against Cambridge in 1954; it was a typically low-key performance though he did bowl steadily, for a while in harness with Ronnie Bell, another local product who never seemed to fit in.

Bick certainly seemed to be knocking on the door for a regular place when early in 1957 he scored three consecutive half centuries when opening the innings against the Universities. Sure enough he was retained for the next two championship games, did little (in common with most of his colleagues) and was out for the season.

All this time his off spin was ignored but at last, in 1959, it was utilised, not regularly, but usefully. Against Yorkshire at Scarborough he achieved his first 5 wicket haul, ripping out the Yorkshire middle batting. Bick never beat this performance. In 1965 Bick actually played 30 matches; his batting return was poor but he did take 61 wickets at 25.01. Not startling but surely a taste of what might have happened given earlier chances. The writing was already on the wall. Fairly regular appearances in 1966 brought slightly less success; this was followed by 3 games in 1967 and that was it.

Bick played for Hertfordshire from 1968 to 1974, and coached at City of London School until his early death. If only? Things that might have been? Did Don Bick himself think that way?

Bernard James Tindal Bosanquet
RHB, LBG, 1898-1919

Born: 13 October 1877, Enfield
Died: 12 October 1936, Ewhurst, Surrey

Batting

M	I	NO	Runs	Av
123	200	13	6593	35.25

50	100	ct/st		
36	13	91		

Bowling

Balls	Runs	Wkts	Av	5wI	10wM
12012	7271	268	27.13	19	6

Best Performances
179 v. Essex at Lord's, 1905
8-53 v. Sussex at Lord's, 1905

Bosanquet started out as a promising all-rounder at Eton and Oxford – an upright, free-hitting batsman and a fast medium bowler – but his developing of what came to be known as the 'googly' or 'Bosie' made him one of cricket history's most romantic figures. The story goes that Bosanquet learned to bowl out of the back of the hand, so an apparent leg break to a right-hand batsman became an off break while playing a game called 'Twistie-Twostie' with a tennis ball. It was said that he obtained the idea from his father, Colonel B.T. Bosanquet, but whatever the true story it seems certain that the first attempted googly in first-class cricket was bowled to Leicestershire batsman Sam Coe at Lord's in 1900. Coe, who was a left-hander so one assumes the intention was a leg break with an off break action, found himself stumped on 98 from a ball which allegedly bounced four times. Whether each bounce was a googly or not is a question not to be asked by anyone valuing his or her sanity, but the Coe dismissal was the start of a long cricket saga.

By 1903/04 it was felt the time was ripe to confront Australia with England's secret weapon. England won the series but only at Sydney in the Fourth Test did Bosanquet produce a match-winning spell. At Trent Bridge in 1905 Australia was destroyed by a second innings analysis of 8 for 107 in 32.4 overs. After 1905 Bosanquet as a Test player was heard of no more. He continued with Middlesex and Gentlemen's teams, ever more haphazardly until 1919 but mainly as a batsman. After 1908 he never took another first-class wicket.

Bosanquet's disciples continued to weave their eccentric spells throughout the twentieth century, but in England in 2002 the art is almost dead. Too much is read into economy, consistency, keeping the batsman quiet. It is not done to 'buy' wickets, nor to entertain the spectator with variations of flight, pace, length, direction and everything else it is possible for a bowler to vary. The advocates of the 'straight up and down' line and length merchants have much to answer for.

As a Middlesex player, Bosanquet's 123 games were marked by outstanding performances. Twice he exceeded 1,000 runs, with 1,103, average 39.39, in 1901 his best effort.

On two occasions he scored a century in each innings of a match, against Leicestershire in 1900 and Sussex in 1905, both at Lord's. Ten of his 13 centuries were in fact made at headquarters. Against Sussex in 1900 he scored exactly 100 runs before lunch. The 227 he added with L.J. Moon against Somerset at Lord's in 1908 remained the county's third-wicket record for 1920.

As an all-rounder Bosanquet on three occasions scored 100 runs and took 10 wickets in a match, against Kent at Tunbridge Wells in 1903, against Yorkshire at Sheffield in 1904 and against Sussex at Lord's in 1905. Only J.W. Hearne has done better. Against Sussex at Hove in 1904 his match-winning analysis was 14 for 190, all on the second day.

Bosanquet himself was something of a dilettante; he rarely if ever had a 'proper' job and when he died left little in the way of money or property to his son Reggie, well known as a television newsreader, known himself for some excesses and eccentricities later in life. But then Bosie could hardly have been expected to father a Stuart Hibberd or Alvar Liddell.

Cartoonist RIP captures 'Bosey' carefully placing his fingers in the correct position for googly, or flipper, or even the boring, conventional leg-break.

John Michael Brearley

RHB, occ. WKT, 1961-1983

Born: 28 April 1942, Harrow

Batting

M	I	NO	Runs	Av
292	485	68	15985	38.33
240	*234*	*28*	*5564*	*27.00*

50	100	ct/st		
85	29	211/1		
34	*3*	*96*		

Bowling

Balls	Runs	Wkts	Av	5wI	10wM
192	119	1	-	-	-
38	*44*	*4*	*11.00*	-	-

Best Performances

173* v. Glamorgan at Cardiff, 1974
124 v. Buckinghamshire at Lord's, 1975*
2-3 v. Northamptonshire at Northampton, 1977

Originally a batsman of outstanding promise, Mike Brearley, the son of a former Yorkshire and Middlesex amateur, never fulfilled early expectations, especially on the international scene, but as a captain, for Middlesex and England he is ranked among the best of all time. Brearley's Test captaincy record – 18 wins and 4 defeats in 31 Tests – is excellent, but his 'home' records – 12 wins and no defeats – is even better. Under his leadership Middlesex won three titles outright and shared another. What is more he took over a shambles and rapidly pulled everything round.

Brearley's very modest Test record (1,442 runs, av. 22.88) tends to lead to his being under-rated as a batsman. In fact his tally of runs and centuries, and his career average, all put him in the top 14 batsmen for the county. Brearley exceeded 1,000 runs in seven seasons, his best return being 1,656 (av. 53.71) in 1975. Against Hampshire at Lord's in 1976 Brearley carried his bat for 128 out of 276 – an admirable solo effort of fortitude when all around him were flinging away their wickets. While not normally associated with fast scoring, against Glamorgan at Cardiff in 1980 Brearley moved from 11 to 124 on the last morning – a superb captain's innings which set up a declaration and eventual victory.

Another fine innings was his 145* against Derbyshire at Derby in 1981, when he and Gatting added 338 together, the third best for the county's third wicket and the best stand for any wicket and either side in the series of fixtures, while Brearley's share of a second wicket stand of 209 with Radley against Worcestershire at Lord's in 1977 was 152. Brearley's best score for Middlesex, however, was a match-deciding unbeaten 173 in more than 5 hours against Glamorgan at Cardiff in 1974. So many of Brearley's county runs came when much needed.

In all first-class cricket Brearley scored 25,185 runs, average 37.81, with a marvellous best score of 312* in 330 minutes for MCC Under-25's against North Zone at Peshawar in 1966/67. He captained the side on this tour, and had skippered Cambridge in 1963/64. At Cambridge he supplemented his value to the side by keeping wicket, but by the time he played regularly for Middlesex he had given up this facet of the game.

If Brearley's cricketing successes owed as much to application, thoroughness, hard work and even intellect as natural flair (though natural ability is essential for any on-field achievements), he was highly gifted academically. The story of his keeping wicket for Cambridge and attempting to disconcert the batsman by discussing philosophical matters with his first slip Eddie Craig is possibly apocryphal (a new, superior form of 'sledging'?) but he did achieve a first in classics. In academic achievement he was probably the equal of C.B. Fry, while in the actual application of knowledge he almost certainly exceeded Fry.

Brearley has lately been in the businesss of applied psychology. He is also a fairly prolific author who has lately been somewhat disappointing in his views and utterances and shows signs of losing touch with the current cricket scene.

J.M. Brearley's studied batting style.

Keith Robert Brown
RHB, WKT, 1984-1998

Born: 18 March 1963, Edmonton

Batting

M	I	NO	Runs	Av
247	373	75	10487	35.19
243	211	51	4549	28.43

50	100	ct/st
56	13	467/33
13	4	167/49

Bowling

Balls	Runs	Wkts	Av	5wI	10wM
321	276	6	46.00	-	-
40	37	0	-	-	-

Best Performances
200* v. Nottinghamshire at Lord's, 1990
114 v. Sussex at Lord's, 1998
2-7 v. Gloucestershire at Bristol, 1987

Keith Brown was a forceful, sometimes belligerent batsman who, in his earlier years at least, was noticeably under-appreciated by the county authorities, especially when it came to choosing teams for important limited-overs games.

In 1990 Brown finally won a regular place and he showed admirable middle-order ability, able to attack or defend according to need, scoring 1,405 runs, average 53.75. Against Nottinghamshire at Lord's he scored his only double century – exactly 200 not out in 6 hours, he and Ramprakash putting the visitors under the cosh with a stand of 188 in 58 overs. A further string was added to Brown's bow when in 1992 he became number 1 wicketkeeper and after taking a season to 'bed in' Brown became arguably the most successful genuine batsman-wicketkeeper the county has ever had. From 1992 until his retirement in 1998, Brown was ever-present in the championship, and showed unerring consistency and reliability both in batting and 'keeping. The best of several good seasons was 1997, when to 917 runs (av. 35.26) and 8 half-centuries he added 61 dismissals. In 18 games this was indeed a fine performance.

The highest of several good stands involving Brown was 268 for the fourth wicket with Gatting against Nottinghamshire at Lord's in 1988, when Brown achieved his maiden hundred. He also added 258 with the same player for the third wicket against Derbyshire at Lord's in 1991.

Behind the stumps Brown proved he was more than a padded-up fielder with such performances as 4 stumpings in the innings against Surrey at The Oval in 1992, one short of the Middlesex best, and a record equalling 8 catches in the match against Glamorgan at Lord's in 1996. After early difficulties he finished his career as only the sixth Middlesex wicketkeeper with 500 dismissals, while only he and Murray have scored 10,000 runs while exceeding 500 dismissals.

Brown did his bit in limited-overs matches; his best performance came against Sussex in the 1998 Benson and Hedges when as an emergency opener his 117 was vital to his side's 6-run victory.

After the 1998 season Brown took up an appointment as a school sportsmaster, an understandable decision, but his retirement seemed to come while he was at his peak and in some circles caused surprise.

Sydney Maurice Brown
RHB, 1937-1955

Born: 8 December 1917, Eltham, Kent
Died: 28 December 1987, Rickmansworth, Herts

Batting

M	I	NO	Runs	Av
313	549	39	15050	29.51
50	100	ct/st		
78	20	146		

Bowling

Balls	Runs	Wkts	Av	5wI	10wM
135	80	3	26.66	-	-

Best Performances
232* v. Somerset at Lord's, 1951
2-19 v. Sussex at Hove, 1951

Syd Brown was one of several fine young batsmen whose burgeoning career was interrupted by the Second World War. On the resumption of cricket in 1946, however, Brown quickly became established as Jack Robertson's opening partner, his attacking style contrasting admirably with Robertson's generally more cultured approach. Their nine opening stands of a century played a large part in the 1947 triumphs. Brown totalled 1,990 runs, average 40.61 for Middlesex during that season. It remained his best.

Brown continued until 1955 but became somewhat inconsistent. Large innings were interspersed with some very barren runs. He found increasing trouble against the moving ball; Brown's style depended overmuch perhaps on a good eye and as his vision lost its keenness and, incidentally, counties in general began to rely more heavily on 'seam', his form was affected. He remained a popular member of the side, however: his superb outfielding in particular endeared him to the spectators. Finding his average reduced to the low twenties in 1955 Brown batted usefully in the county's final match and then, wisely,

announced his retirement. His subsequent cricket was for Kenton.

Syd Brown exceeded 1,000 runs for the county nine times, his best being 1,990 in 1947. The first of his 20 centuries came against Lancashire in 1938 when aged 20. Twice he was to go on to a double century. Brown's generally aggressive approach was illustrated against Essex at Westcliff in 1946 when he reached his century on the first morning during his knock of 118. Against Cambridge at Fenner's in 1948 he dominated matters during an all-out 153 as he carried his bat unbeaten for 96.

Brown and Robertson were an opening pair with an unusual propensity for high stands. Their best was an epic 310, a county first-wicket record for twenty years, against Notts at Lord's in 1947. On four further occasions the pair exceeded 200 for the first wicket while Brown also twice added more than 200 with Harry Sharp. In 1954, after Robertson's early demise Brown and Bill Edrich put on 324 for the second wicket, against Warwickshire at Edgbaston. This is still the best stand for either side, and any wicket in the series of matches.

Charles Francis Buller

RHB, RA slow, 1865-1877

C.F. Buller was one of the most brilliant schoolboy cricketers of his day, being four years in the XI at Eton, as well as being a fine athlete. A batsman with a wide array of strokes and an apparently innate sense of timing, he immediately made an impact when first tried at the age of nineteen, scoring a superb unbeaten 105 against Surrey at Islington in his second match. He remains the fourth youngest century-maker for the county; the next best score was 31 and Buller played a huge part in Middlesex's win. The 88 Buller added with I.D. Walker was a seventh-wicket record for the county at the time. A few days earlier, Buller had top scored with 73 in a first-class match for a Gentlemen of Middlesex side against Gentlemen of England at Islington. The England side included another precocious teenager, W.G. Grace. They scored a similar number of runs and Buller was in no way outshone. The previous season, when just eighteen, Buller had scored 68 for Gentlemen of MCC *v.* Gentlemen of Kent at Canterbury. It was the top score for either side. His promise seemed infinite. Buller showed good form the following season and for MCC against Sussex at Lord's obtained his highest-ever score, 106, by a long way the best of the match. He was just twenty when he was gazetted into the 2nd Life Guards and played little for several years, returning after leaving the forces in 1874. Sadly as a cricketer he was a mere shadow of the boy genius, who first played for Devon and

Born: 26 May 1846, Colombo, Ceylon (Sri Lanka)

Died: 22 November 1906, Lyme Regis, Dorset

Batting

M	I	NO	Runs	Av
24	44	4	870	21.75
50	100	ct/st		
1	1	8		

Bowling

Balls	Runs	Wkts	Av	5wl	10wM
52	32	0	-	-	-

Best Performances

205* v. Surrey at The Oval, 1865

Cornwall at Plymouth against the England XI aged 14. Loose living (and loving) had converted the slim teenager into an overweight and ponderous 'twenty-something'. His batting had deteriorated, his lack of speed found him a liability in the field and by 1877 his first-class career was at an end, a final record of 3,140 runs (21.80) proving a big disappointment.

When touching upon 'the scandals that marred Mr Buller's private life and caused his social eclipse', *Wisden* in his obituary describes Buller as 'perhaps the handsomest man the cricket field has known.' Strangely and disappointingly, it has been very hard to find a decent likeness for this book.

Middlesex CCC, 1878. From left to right, back row: M. Flanagan, A. Burghes, Mr Hewitt (umpire), C.J. Lucas, M.T. Turner, R. Henderson, C.F. Buller. Front row: W.H. Hadow, A.J. Webbe, I.D. Walker, J.W. Dale, H.R. Webbe.

George Burton
RHB, RA slow, 1881-1893

Born: 1 May 1851, Hampstead
Died: 7 May 1930, Covent Garden, London

Batting

M	I	NO	Runs	Av
111	176	54	946	7.75
50	100	ct/st		
-	-	90		

Bowling

Balls	Runs	Wkts	Av	5wl	10wM
26926	9079	529	17.16	43	10

Best Performances
34 v. Nottinghamshire at Lord's, 1881
10-59 v. Surrey at The Oval, 1888

George 'Farmer' Burton was a splendid round-arm bowler with break either way, a true Londoner and one of the best and most respected professionals of his day. Burton started off as a member of Islington Youths' Institute Cricket Club; other clubs were Bedford Amateurs, Upper Holloway, Holborn and North Middlesex. After retirement he became Middlesex scorer and also saw service as an umpire. From 1883 to 1904 he was on the Lord's coaching staff, and earned a high reputation. Until his death, Burton was Hon. Secretary of the Cricketers' Fund Friendly Society. Outside cricket Burton plied his trade as a coachsmith while his excellent tenor voice made him a regular soloist at Christ Church, Lancaster Gate. Burton, whose son Frederick Alfred was also on the Lord's staff and played for Hertfordshire, appears to have been a credit to himself and to cricket, and also to the old-fashioned 'London professional', a genus which no longer seems to exist.

George Burton was, for much of his career, the best bowler in the side. His biggest triumph came in the Surrey match at The Oval in 1888 when he took all 10 first-innings wickets for 59, the first 'all-10' by a Middlesex bowler. Burton was the only professional and his amateur colleagues somehow contrived to lose the match. He reached his peak in this season. In the following game, again as the lone professional, his match figures of 16 for 114 helped defeat Yorkshire at Bramall Lane. In May he had match figures of 10 for 71 as the 'Tykes' were beaten at Lord's. In 13 matches for the county in 1888, he took 87 wickets, average 11.5. It was a minor mystery why he did not appear against Australia this season, especially in the Lord's Test when the team was chosen by MCC and England were beaten.

Apart from his 'all-10', George Burton took 8 wickets in an innings four times, and 7 in an innings on five occasions. His 16 for 114 match figures against Yorkshire in 1888 remain the county's best analysis; perhaps he was as proud of his 14 for 192 against the 1886 Australians. Burton was the first bowler to take 500 wickets for Middlesex; they remain the cheapest.

Roland Orlando Butcher

RHB, 1974-1990

Born: 14 October 1953, East Point, St Philip, Barbados

Batting

M	I	NO	Runs	Av
251	383	38	10935	31.69
257	232	25	4640	22.41

50	100	ct/st
59	17	265
25	1	81

Bowling

Balls	Runs	Wkts	Av	5wI	10wM
261	161	4	40.25	-	-
20	23	1	-	-	-

Best Performances

197 v. Yorkshire at Lord's, 1982
100 v. Gloucestershire at Lord's, 1983
2-37 v. Gloucestershire at Cheltenham, 1986

Roland Butcher, West Indian-born but who had resided in England since the age of thirteen was somewhat surprisingly chosen for England in 1980 – but even more inexplicably discarded permanently after a mere three Test matches, another victim of English selectorial eccentricities. Butcher remained a valuable if somewhat inconsistent member of the Middlesex team for more than a decade, an aggressive and sometimes quite thrilling stroke player capable of winning matches or at least giving opposition bowlers and captains heart failure. He was also a brilliant field and occasionally kept wicket to a standard somewhat short of the highest class.

A facial injury incurred while batting against Leicestershire at Lord's in 1984 – he was hit trying to hook Leicestershire's paceman George Ferris – affected his play for some time and eye trouble forced him to bat in spectacles, but he remained a dangerous player for his county until 1990, when he retired from the first-class game and joined Cambridgeshire.

Butcher exceeded 1,000 runs four times for the county. By far the most notable of his 20 centuries was his 171 against Surrey at Uxbridge in 1986. Going in on the first evening, at the close he was 12 not out. On the second morning, he raced to his century in 95 balls and scored 125 of his county's 165 pre-lunch runs. He finally hit 25 fours and 3 sixes in a magnificent exhibition on an unreliable pitch. Sadly Butcher finished up on the losing side. Another great innings was his 197 against Yorkshire at Lord's in 1982. With quick runs sought towards a second-evening declaration, and in variable light Butcher hit 6 sixes in an innings which became ever more savage. He and Gatting added 237 for the fourth wicket, 156 was then put on for the fifth wicket with Emburey before, with a declaration pending, Butcher ran himself out only 3 short of what would have been his only double century. Rain the following day condemned the game to a draw. Butcher seems to have been the unlucky type whose best efforts somehow never brought the deserved reward.

John Donald Carr
RHB, OB, 1983-1996

Born: 15 June 1963, St John's Wood

Batting

M	I	NO	Runs	Av
191	300	51	9846	39.54
181	169	26	4705	32.90
50	100	ct/st		
45	20	243		
18	2	84		

Bowling

Balls	Runs	Wkts	Av	5wI	10wM
2651	1156	33	35.03	1	-
1764	1258	43	29.25	-	-

Best Performances
261* v. Gloucestershire at Lord's, 1994
106 v. Gloucestershire at Lord's, 1996
6-61 v. Gloucestershire at Lord's, 1985
4-21 v. Surrey at Lord's, 1989

John Carr enjoyed a remarkable Middlesex career. The son of Derbyshire and England skipper and sometime Lord's luminary Donald Carr, he initially showed great promise as an all-rounder, winning his Blue at Oxford but in his first few seasons with Middlesex his batting developed as his bowling declined. Technical problems saw Carr actually leave the staff for a time but he returned with a batting method so much changed it seemed more suited to a baseball match and in 1994 had one of the most remarkable seasons of any Middlesex batters. Carr actually scored 1,543 runs for an average of 90.76, and made 7 centuries, with a best of 261 not out from 289 balls against Gloucestershire at Lord's in the season's penultimate match. On the way Carr and Paul Weekes added 270 together, a new Middlesex sixth-wicket record. Carr seemed to bat well with Weekes, since that same season the pair put on 264 against Somerset, second all-time for the Middlesex seventh wicket but the best at Lord's for or against the county. Perhaps the most remarkable facet of

Carr's season in 1994 was his phenomenal run after the birth of his daughter in August – 78*, 171*, 136 and 106* (he and Gatting added 282* for the fourth wicket against Northamptonshire at Northampton), 40* and 62*, 261*. The following season the spell was broken, though he still batted well, but the magic had gone in 1996 and at the season's end he retired.

John Carr may sometimes be regarded as a 'one season wonder' but the statistics suggest otherwise. His Middlesex career total of 9,846 runs brought an average of 39.54 and 20 centuries. He exceeded 1,000 runs five times and as early as 1987 scored 111 not out by lunch on the first day of the Surrey game at Lord's.

Carr's Oxford days helped him to a career total of 10,895 runs, average 38.91. He caught excellently for 268 victims; his latterly little-used seamers brought 68 wickets. So many other players were given England chances in Carr's time he can perhaps regard himself as unfortunate that he missed the boat when at his best.

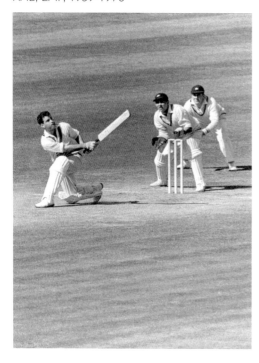

Born: 15 April 1937, Balham, S. London

Batting

M	I	NO	Runs	Av
196	332	39	8595	29.33
9	9	1	220	27.50

50	100	ct/st
51	6	105
1	-	1

Bowling

Balls	Runs	Wkts	Av	5wI	10wM
3617	1822	58	31.41	2	-
224	166	6	27.66	-	-

Best Performances
149 v. Kent at Gravesend, 1966
51 v. Lancashire at Lord's, 1966
5-61 v. Surrey at The Oval, 1961
2-49 v. Surrey at The Oval, 1964

Ted Clark was born south of the Thames, in Balham, but played his club cricket in north London, mainly for Spencer and Teddington. He started on the very highest of notes when he scored 100 not out in a couple of hours on his first-class debut. The match was against Cambridge University at Fenner's in 1959; the bowling, led by Alan Wheelhouse and Alan Hurd, was hardly the most fearsome on the circuit, but he showed style and polish. Strangely, Clark was immediately left out of the side, not to return until July when he showed more signs of quality, notably against Northamptonshire at Lord's when his scores of 121 and 73* were the only scores of more than 50 for his side and most certainly saved the match. Ted Clark was already twenty-two; he showed flair and an ability to score runs when required but he needed to play regularly, not be pushed around. His treatment seems sadly typical of English cricket attitudes. Back trouble subsequently hindered his development, and perhaps shortened his cricketing life. Surprisingly for one of his class he scored only 6 centuries despite making 57 half-centuries – thus showing a disappointing vulnerability for big scores – but he did exceed 1,000 runs in five seasons, with a best of 1,454 (average 32.31) in 1964 and perhaps his early retirement after 1966 to enter business came as a surprise. Clark briefly emerged from retirement in 1976 – a strange happening given his age (thirty-nine) and the need to build for the future.

In addition to his batting, Ted Clark also bowled quick medium left arm with sufficient life and, in helpful conditions, fire to twice take 5 in an innings, yet seemed to be startlingly underused. He had a heating engineering business after retirement. In 1981 he became an MCC committee member, an accolade which admitted him to cricket's great and good. Yet, one cannot but remember the batsman with the apparent style and touch to take him to the top. For whatever reason he never reached the level demanded by his natural ability.

Denis Charles Scott Compton
RHB, SLA, 1936-1958

Born: 23 May 1918, Hendon
Died: 23 April 1997, Windsor, Berks.

Batting

M	I	NO	Runs	Av
296	485	49	21781	49.95

50	100	ct/st
104	67	264

Bowling

Balls	Runs	Wkts	Av	5wI	10wM
26564	14124	477	29.61	16	2

Best Performances
252* v. Somerset at Lord's, 1948
6-63 v. Gloucestershire at Lord's, 1952

Denis Compton made his debut as a slow-bowling deputy for Peebles against Sussex in 1936. Two weeks later at Northampton, Compton scored 100* in 106 minutes before lunch on the third day, kick-starting the career of the most brilliant batsman ever to play for Middlesex.

At his best Compton played with such carefree ease, often seeming deliberately to pick the right stroke for the wrong ball just to show himself it could be done, that it is in a way surprising that his record is so impressive statistically. His 21,781 runs put him eighth on the Middlesex list, an average of 49.95 places him second, with 67 hundreds he is fourth, but at one every 7.23 innings he comes top.

Compton exceeded 1,000 runs in 12 seasons. In 1946 he stretched this to 2,042 (av. 65.87) but this was overshadowed by his record in 1947. For Middlesex Compton scored 2,467 (av. 102.79) and in all cricket an unprecedented and unapproachable 3,816 (av. 90.85). He scored a Middlesex record 13 centuries, and 18 in all first-class matches. These are season records which will probably survive cricket.

Compton scored 5 double centuries for Middlesex, the biggest being 252* in only 4 hours against Somerset at Lord's in 1948. He and Edrich added an unbroken 424 for the third wicket; this remains a Middlesex record for any wicket. In 1947 he had scored 246 against The Rest at The Oval, his 18th and final hundred of the season, a brilliant knock despite knee trouble. In 1946 his 235 against Surrey at Lord's occupied only 280 minutes and with Edrich he added 296 for the third wicket. The pair also added 287 unbroken for the third wicket against Surrey at The Oval in 1947 and 277 for the second wicket against Leicestershire at Leicester in the same season. Compton also enjoyed a fourth-wicket stand of 304 in 195 minutes with George Mann against Surrey at Lord's in 1947.

In all first-class cricket Compton scored 38,942 runs, average 51.83, with 123 centuries, and a best of 300 in 181 minutes (the fastest ever triple century) for MCC v. North-East Transvaal at Benoni in 1948/49. He held 416 catches and even though his bowling unsurprisingly never really developed he still took 622 wickets. In Tests he had 5,807 runs (50.06) with 17 centuries, the best being a

27

Denis Compton – 200 not out at Trent Bridge in 1954.

brilliant 278 in 290 minutes against Pakistan at Trent Bridge in 1954.

Compton is remembered for his range of often strictly personal attacking strokes, the most famous being the sweep which was played to any type of ball with complete confidence. He also had his own version of the leg glance (more a flick) and the off drive which would send the ball scudding to the boundary with minimal effort. Compton's secrets were a good eye, cheerful self-confidence, a surprisingly sound and orthodox defence, plus a touch of genius. Even towards the end of his career when, handicapped by increasing weight and fitness problems he could no longer go on to big scores, his batting still looked 'different'.

After retirement Compton was for many years cricket writer for the *Sunday Express* and a broadcaster. His writings and comments were sometimes surprisingly mundane and, to some people, wrong-headed and ill-advised. He still enjoyed life, however, and his young third wife produced two daughters when her husband was in his sixties.

Leslie Harry Compton
RHB, WKT, RM, 1938-1956

Born: 12 September 1912, Woodford, Essex
Died: 27 December 1984, Hendon

Batting

M	I	NO	Runs	Av
272	389	46	5781	16.85
50	**100**	**ct/st**		
23	1	465/131		

Bowling

Balls	Runs	Wkts	Av	5wI	10wM
1069	569	12	47.42	-	-

Best Performances
107 v. Derbyshire at Derby, 1947
2-21 v. Essex at Westcliff, 1946

Leslie Compton was a talented cricketer who found it difficult to find his proper niche in the game, but after the interruption caused by war, he established himself as a safe and surprisingly agile wicketkeeper, as well as one of the biggest ever to play regular county cricket. Les had shown early promise as a batsman and seam bowler but although remaining useful in the former capacity he never seemed to learn which ball to pick and often got himself out unnecessarily. Though war hindered his development it is doubtful whether his medium pacers would ever have been more than occasionally useful. Notwithstanding his disappointments in other departments of the game, Les Compton was a good enough wicketkeeper not to be known as 'Denis Compton's brother'.

Les Compton's most prolific wicketkeeping season was 1947. His 78 dismissals had at the time been exceeded by only two Middlesex wicketkeepers. His career total of 596 put him fourth all-time for the county. He is one of six wicketkeepers to total 5,000 runs and 500 dis-

missals for Middlesex. Compton's batting was never above the 'useful' category, partly due to the war which so cruelly delayed his career, but until his eye began to deteriorate he played a number of aggressive innings which usually featured hard and sure driving. His only century, 107 against Derbyshire at Derby in 1947, came in 95 minutes. He added 181 for the fifth wicket with Syd Brown; it was a match-winning stand for a side lacking Robertson and Denis Compton.

Les Compton, who during the war played for London Counties, was an all-round sportsman. As a rugged and brave centre half for Arsenal who liked nothing better than a 'battle' with one of the many 'forceful' centre forwards of his time, he won two England caps in his thirty-eighth year. In later years a popular Boniface in North London, he never recovered health or spirit after amputation of part of a leg.

To return finally to his cricket: the legend that he was run out for 1 by his brother in his benefit match against Sussex at Lord's in 1954 appears to be true.

Norman George Cowans
RHB, RFM, 1980-1993

Born: 17 April 1961, Enfield St Mary, Jamaica

Batting

M	I	NO	Runs	Av
188	190	49	1307	19.26
168	61	20	234	5.70

50	100	ct/st
1	-	47
-	-	30

Bowling

Balls	Runs	Wkts	Av	5wI	10wM
24427	12009	532	22.57	18	1
8256	5122	206	24.86	1	-

Best Performances
66 v. Surrey at Lord's, 1984
27 v. Nottinghamshire at Lord's, 1990
6-31 v. Leicestershire at Leicester, 1985
6-9 v. Lancashire at Lord's, 1991

Tall and loose-limbed, with a good turn of speed, Norman Cowans seemed to be the answer to a Middlesex and England prayer as a quick bowler of genuine quality. Nevertheless, subsequent doubts, some perhaps in his own mind, about his fitness and stamina probably prevented his reaching the hoped-for high standards. Although from around 1991 there was a marked reduction in his pace, Cowans gave valuable service to county and country.

Cowans, born in Jamaica but reared in North London, first played for Middlesex at Oxford in 1980. He was used sparingly however, and despite a match-winning spell of 5 for 58 in 13 overs against Leicestershire in late 1981, not until 1982 was he given proper opportunities to show his worth at the highest level of county cricket.

Cowans was already an England player at Test and limited overs level when he at last showed consistent quality in the county game in 1984, taking a personal record of 71 wick-

ets, average 19.52. Among some fine performances that season, none was better than a first innings analysis of 6 for 64 against Warwickshire at Lord's, when an early spell of 4 for 6 decimated the Midland county's hesitant early batting. It was hardly Cowans' fault that his side, mainly due to its own timorous batting, lost the match.

Another fine season followed in 1985, his 65 wickets including a career best 6 for 31 at Leicester when hostile pace from him and Wayne Daniel shattered the home side, and in 1988 he equalled his best-ever return with 71 wickets (18.16). At Uxbridge his career-best figures of 10 for 97 shattered Warwickshire. As injury and stiffening sinews took their toll a gentle downturn then hit Cowans' career and he played no more after 1993. His had been a good and useful career, yet somehow disappointing, as career figures for all first-class cricket of 1,531 runs, average 9.16, and 620 wickets, average 24.58, and Test bowling figures of 51 wickets for the high average of 39.27 tend to confirm.

Wayne Wendel Daniel
RHB, RF, 1977-1988

Born: 16 January 1956, St Philip, Barbados

Batting

M	I	NO	Runs	Av
214	187	86	1043	10.32
205	76	31	220	4.88

50	100	ct/st
1	-	52
-	-	30

Bowling

Balls	Runs	Wkts	Av	5wI	10wM
30053	15089	685	22.02	22	4
9753	5470	315	17.36	17	-

Best Performances
53* v. Yorkshire at Lord's, 1981
20 v. Derbyshire at Derby, 1978*
9-61 v. Glamorgan at Swansea, 1982
7-12 v. Minor Counties East at Ipswich, 1978

Wayne Daniel came to Middlesex with a reputation as a fearsome fast bowler but possibly a suspect temperament. Any doubts about him however were quickly proved to be unfounded. His bowling fully lived up to its promise but as a person Daniel became one of the most popular of all overseas county players, whose nickname 'The Black Diamond' was completely justified. In his years of service to the county, Daniel, tall and strong, fast and straight, bowled himself into the ground for Middlesex. He was indeed one of the best overseas imports for any county.

Daniel was capped immediately in 1977 and he celebrated his new career with 75 wickets at 16.44. 76 wickets (14.65) followed in 1978 and as late as 1985 he achieved a career best 79 wickets, at an admittedly higher than usual average, 26.72. When the years of unflinching service took their final toll in 1988 Daniel had exceeded 50 wickets in a season on 9 occasions and until his last season he had hardly missed a match through injury.

Daniel's best bowling figure for the county was 9 for 61 against Glamorgan at Swansea in 1982. Daniel had match figures of 11 for 97 in 37 overs and the hostile bowling of him and Gatting sent the home side racing to a humiliating defeat. The following season Daniel, with match figures of 10 for 61 in partnership with Simon Hughes sent Gloucestershire plunging to an innings defeat at Bristol, while in 1985 Daniel's second innings figures of 7 for 62 at Leicester set up the home county for a 10-wicket defeat. Daniel enjoyed many other fine feats but it was his consistency as a fast and aggressive bowler who was rarely injured which marks him down as a Middlesex hero.

Daniel took 867 first-class wickets at an average of 22.47 and scored 1,151 runs. In international cricket Daniel had to compete with some of the finest West Indian pacemen of all time. His record – 36 wickets at 25.27 – is perhaps disappointing but Middlesex had no complaints that he reserved his best for them.

John Gordon Dewes
LHB, 1948-1956

Born: 11 October 1926, North Latchford, Cheshire

Batting

M	I	NO	Runs	Av
62	102	8	3589	38.18
50	100	ct/st		
17	10	21		

Bowling

Balls	Runs	Wkts	Av	5wI	10wM
24	10	1	-	-	-

Best Performances
139 v. Yorkshire at Headingley, 1950

John Dewes' first-class debut aged eighteen in 1945 was for Engand v. Australia. At Cambridge after exceeding 1,000 runs in May he gained what was still a wartime Blue.

Back at Cambridge in 1948 after National Service, he established such a propensity for big scores and massive partnerships he seemed marked down for future success. In 1949 Dewes (204) and Hubert Doggart added 429 against Essex at Fenner's – at the time the best second-wicket stand in English domestic cricket. In 1950 Dewes (212) put on 349 for a Cambridge first-wicket record with D.S. Sheppard. The pair also added 343 in 280 minutes against the all-conquering West Indians. Yet when given Test opportunities, he was dismissed in single figures 7 times in 10 starts, while in his only Test tour, to Australia in 1950/51, he struggled throughout. With a method based upon very sound defence and a range of wristy scoring shots, and coached as a boy by his father never to lift the ball, Dewes should have done better.

Dewes never did a full season with Middlesex. His studies and teaching meant late summer was the only time he could appear. He carried on until 1956, despite uncertain fitness and a manifest lack of proper practice, and his results suggested a lot of lost left-handed runs.

Despite irregular appearances his century rate of one in 10 innings is beaten among the County's English players only by Denis Compton, Hendren, Gatting and Ramprakash which is a remarkable statistic in any circumstances. Against Sussex in 1950 he scored a century in each innings, part of a run of 4 centuries in 7 innings. He pulled and drove with great confidence and dominated two large opening stand with Robertson. It was also a match decisive performance. As late as 1955 Dewes carried his bat for 101 out of 203 against Surrey's strongest attack, a five-hour effort which prevented disaster. Dewes scored 35 in the second innings; no other Middlesex batsman exceeded 24 in the whole match. In 1949, against the New Zealand tourists Dewes added 210 with Denis Compton. Things to come? But they never did. Cricket's loss was the gain of academia.

Born: 8 January 1870, Norwood Green, Southall
Died: 8 February 1958, Cheltenham, Glos.

Batting

M	I	NO	Runs	Av
164	277	20	7669	29.84
50	100	ct/st		
31	13	151		

Bowling

Balls	Runs	Wkts	Av	5wI	10wM
1162	672	17	39.52	1	-

Best Performances
204 v. Gloucestershire at Bristol, 1903
5-98 v. Sussex at Lord's, 1893

James Douglas, whose brothers Archibald Philip, Robert Noel and Sholto also played for Middlesex, was a well-taught, basically orthodox and extremely sound batsman but could sometimes improvise to good effect. In his youth, Douglas was also a good left-arm bowler with little spin but who varied pace and length to good effect. His fielding away from the bat was brilliant.

Douglas won his Blue at Cambridge, for whom his most memorable performance was probably taking 5 wickets for 45 against the 1893 Australians. He subsequently played for Middlesex for many years, but almost exclusively during the school holidays, as he was a schoolmaster at Dulwich and later his own school, Hillside in Godalming.

Considering his lack of regular practice, Douglas performed extremely well to score 13 centuries, the highest of which was 204 in 315 minutes against Gloucestershire at Bristol in 1903. He was in century stands with his skipper Gregor McGregor and C.M. Wells and played a notable part in his side's win. Perhaps even better was his magnificent 153 in 3 hours against Nottinghamshire at Trent Bridge the following season. Douglas and P.F. Warner added 306, the county first-wicket record until 1947. Douglas and Warner had scored 218 for the first wicket against Lancashire in 1901, and in 1907 put on 232 against Surrey at The Oval. Six of Douglas's centuries exceeded 150, suggesting a temperament for high scores.

A score of 114 on the first morning against Somerset at Taunton in 1904 also confirms an ability to score quickly, and there seems little reasonable doubt that regular appearances may have brought runs in the very highest class of cricket.

Finally, it is curious so little was made of his bowling since on his Middlesex debut against Sussex at Lord's in 1893 he had first innings figures of 5 for 98 in 42.5 overs, his victims including Test batsmen W.L. Murdoch and W. Newham. Perhaps it was lack of use which saw him lose the knack.

Paul Rupert Downton

RHB, WKT, 1980-1991

Born: 4 April 1957, Farnborough, Kent

Batting

M	I	NO	Runs	Av
219	291	54	6891	29.07
221	166	48	2892	24.50
50	100	ct/st		
38	6	474/63		
8	-	205/49		

Bowling

Balls	Runs	Wkts	Av	5wI	10wM
55	9	I	-	-	-

Best Performances

126* v. Oxford University at Oxford, 1986
80* v. Hampshire at Southampton, 1987

Paul Downton played for his native Kent, following his father George, before joining Middlesex where he quickly won Test recognition. When moving to Middlesex in 1980 (he felt his hopes of a Test career would be boosted by regular appearances at Lord's) Downton supplanted the popular Ian Gould, but he supplied a decade of valuable service before an eye injury forced his premature retirement. Downton was a busy and businesslike cricketer, lively and active behind the stumps with a style ideally suited to limited-overs cricket. His 'keeping was highly regarded by John Murray among others and, if he did not quite reach the heights some no doubt expected of him, he was usually good enough. Although not top-class with the bat, he was held in sufficient regard to open the county's batting on occasions.

Downton, who was capped in 1981 and received a benefit in 1990, usually showed a safe pair of hands, illustrated when he took 6 catches in an innings and 8 in the match against Nottinghamshire at Trent Bridge in

1981. Although a reduced fixture list was a handicap, his total of 537 dismissals puts him 5th among the county's 'keepers and his average of dismissals per match compares favourably with any of the top Middlesex wicketkeepers.

Downton's best batting season was 1987, when he scored 1,052 runs, average 36.27. This was his only 1,000-run season but he scored 6 centuries for the county during his career. The highest was 126* against Oxford in 1986 but the best was probably his 120 in 270 minutes against Lancashire at Old Trafford in 1988. He was the only batsman on either side to exceed 50 and played a huge part in a 10-wicket win.

A first-class record of 8,270 runs (av. 25.13) and 779 dismissals in a curtailed career speaks much for Downton's quality as a cricketer. 785 runs (av. 19.62) and 75 dismissals in 30 Tests is more reminiscent of a wicketkeeper who scored useful runs rather than a batsman-keeper, but he was very useful for all that.

Frederick John Durston
RHB, RFM, OB, 1919-1933

Born: 11 July 1893, Clophill, Bedfordshire
Died: 8 April 1965, Norwood Green, Southall

Batting

M	I	NO	Runs	Av
349	434	127	3569	11.62
50	**100**	**ct/st**		
2	-	230		

Bowling

Balls	Runs	Wkts	Av	5wl	10wM
64933	25877	1178	21.96	65	7

Best Performances
92* v. Northamptonshire at Lord's, 1930
8-27 v. Oxford University at Oxford, 1923

Jack Durston, a Bedfordshire village lad, joined the Lord's staff in 1914 but his first-class career was then put on hold until the cessation of hostilities.

Standing 6ft 4in high, Durston used his great height to good effect. He gained lift at a brisk pace and also had an effective break-back. Initially very slim, Durston began to put on weight in his thirties. This affected his abilities as a fast bowler but he changed to off spin with fairly good effect. Originally a pretty poor bat, Jack Durston eventually learned to hit hard with discrimination and became a useful tail-ender, swinging his bat effectively against bowlers anxious to take their between-innings break. His capacious hands caught most things within reach.

On ten occasions Jack Durston took 7 or more wickets in an innings – nearly as many as Edmonds and Emburey put together. His best analysis statistically was a match-winning 8 for 27 against Oxford in the Parks in 1923. Weeks later he took the first 8 wickets in Gloucestershire's second innings – and fin-

ished with 8 for 56 to win the game. Possibly Durston himself preferred the innings analysis of 7 for 133 against Yorkshire at Lord's in 1928. He was by now slower and more subtle, and it followed 8 for 40 against Essex at Leyton only days earlier.

Durston exceeded 100 wickets in a season four times, and the first was the best. He bowled magnificently in 1920 to take 111 wickets, average 20.96, and played a big though understated part in his side's championship success. Against Northamptonshire at Lord's in 1930 Durston enjoyed a batting triumph. In the first innings his 51 took less than an hour but in the second innings, given some batting promotion, he settled to an unbeaten 92 in 150 minutes and added 99 for the sixth wicket with Haig.

After retirement Durston remained on the Lord's staff and umpired a number of games at headquarters. He played for Hounslow and during the Second World War turned out for London Counties. He also became a respected coach at the Acton cricket school.

Phillipe Henri Edmonds

RHB, SLA, 1971-1987

Born: 8 March 1951, Lusaka, N. Rhodesia (Zambia)

Batting

M	I	NO	Runs	Av
257	311	57	5036	19.82
252	184	47	2184	15.94

50	100	ct/st
16	2	227
2	-	77

Bowling

Balls	Runs	Wkts	Av	5wl	10wM
55678	20803	883	23.55	39	8
10575	6766	286	23.65	6	-

Best Performances

142 v. Glamorgan at Swansea, 1984
63* v. Somerset at Lord's, 1979
8-53 v. Hampshire at Bournemouth, 1984
5-12 v. Cheshire at Enfield, 1982

Phil Edmonds was an infuriating cricketer. He was tall and richly gifted as a left-armed spinner with good action and superb control and an aggressive batsman capable of big centuries as well as a brave close fieldsman. However, his contrary and argumentative nature saw him make important cricket enemies as well as probably affecting his own performances. Thus his career was probably curtailed prematurely and his reputation owed as much to his personality as his undoubted ability.

Edmonds became a Middlesex regular after captaining Cambridge and despite its vicissitudes his career was one of great usefulness. In batting, his 2 centuries were both big, and both against Glamorgan. The best of several useful late-order stands was the 160 he added with Gatting for the seventh wicket against Northamptonshire at Lord's in 1976. *Wisden* states that Edmonds 'hit violently' for 93 in 89 minutes. He also counted 4 sixes among his scoring strokes.

Edmonds' best and certainly most effective bowling for Middlesex came against Hampshire at Bournemouth in 1984. His first innnings 4 for 67 in 29.2 overs kept things in check; his devastating 8 for 53 in 32 overs in the second innings shattered the home side. Almost single-handedly Edmonds put his side into a winning position, which was then used to advantage despite uncertain weather. Against Leicestershire at Leicester in 1981, Edmonds took three top-order batsmen as his first-innings hat-trick. Having set things up, he did little in the rest of a match which saw an innings victory.

Phil Edmonds played 51 Tests, scoring 976 runs (17.50) and taking 125 wickets (34.18); useful figures indeed, but they should have been better. His batting disappointed while his bowling often tended towards the mechanical. After retirement he wrote *Phil Edmonds' 100 Great Bowlers* – interesting in places but non-controversial and at times disappointly predictable. After this, he had a short career as a television commentator.

William John Edrich
RHB, RFM, OB, 1937-1958

Born: 26 March 1916, Lingwood, Norfolk
Died: 24 April 1986, Chesham, Bucks.

Batting

M	I	NO	Runs	Av
389	658	65	25738	43.40

50	100	ct/st		
135	62	382/1		

Bowling

Balls	Runs	Wkts	Av	5wI	10wM
21693	9975	328	30.41	10	1

Best Performances
267* v. Northamptonshire at Northampton, 1947
7-48 v. Worcestershire at Worcester, 1946

Square built and short, Bill Edrich had the power of a sawn-off shotgun. He employed the hook, the pull and the drive fiercely, positively and with enormous confidence but his method was based on sound principles.

He scored 1,000 runs in 1937, his first season, and in 1938 had scored 1,000 runs by the end of May, all at Lord's, though not all for Middlesex. His peak was reached in 1947 when Edrich and Compton broke most of the batting records in the sun-strewn Championship year. Though never repeating his 1947 form, Edrich remained a valuable batsman and from 1953 to 1957 he captained Middlesex. It was a difficult period, but he led the county conscientiously if somewhat conventionally. Finally, he returned to Norfolk, whence he came, and captained them for a decade.

Edrich exceeded 1,000 runs in 15 seasons for Middlesex, with a glorious best of 2,654, average 85.48, in 1947. His total stands second only in Middlesex records to Patsy Hendren's 2,669 runs in 1923. In 1939 he had totalled exactly 2,000 runs, average 51.28, and in 1952, 2,101 runs, average 41.19. Another interesting statistic is that Edrich reached his half-century 197 times, and it speaks volumes for his consistency that only Hendren and Gatting beat him.

It is perhaps inevitable that 1947 saw Edrich's two best scores, but strange that neither was at Lord's. Against Leicestershire at Leicester, and leading Middlesex for the first time, Edrich hit 257 in 4 hours and 45 minutes, including 4 sixes, and he and Denis Compton added 277 in 130 marvellous minutes. Little more than a week later Edrich thrashed Northamptonshire at Northampton for an unbeaten 267 in just under 6 hours, with 3 sixes. This time he and Compton added 211. Both matches were well won and it was glorious stuff. Earlier in the season Edrich had scored 225 in 350 minutes; truly it was his great season. Altogether, Edrich scored 8 double centuries, a total beaten only by J.W. Hearne and Hendren.

Most noteworthy of the many large stands involving Edrich was the 424 he and Denis Compton added for the third wicket against Somerset at Lord's in 1948. It remains the Middlesex record for any wicket and the best for any side at Lord's. It took a mere 4 hours of the first day. In 1938, Edrich and Compton

Bill Edrich – 'sawn-off shotgun'.

had added 304 for the same wicket against Gloucestershire at Lord's. Other great third-wicket efforts by the pair were 296 against Surrey at Lord's in 1947 and 287* against the same county at The Oval in 1947. In 1952, Edrich and Alec Thompson added 315 for the second wicket at Dudley and as late as 1954 he and Syd Brown compiled 324 together for the second wicket against Warwickshire at Edgbaston.

It is almost forgotten that Edrich's quick bowling twice brought him 7 wickets in an innings in 1946 and his 382 catches, mainly at slip, is 5th best for Middlesex.

Edrich's first-class career brought him 36,954 runs (av. 42.39), 86 centuries, 529 catches and 479 wickets. In Tests he had 2,440 runs (av. 40.00) and 41 wickets. He was sometimes disappointing yet the record is good, and there is no gainsaying that here was a marvellous cricketer.

Perhaps it is appropriate that this party-loving war hero died after a St George's Day celebration. One hopes he would have approved.

John Ernest Emburey
RHB, OB, 1973-1995

Born: 20 August 1952, Peckham, London

Batting

M	I	NO	Runs	Av
376	464	93	9053	24.40
388	*258*	*83*	*2955*	*16.88*

50	100	ct/st		
40	7	368		
2	*-*	*137*		

Bowling

Balls	Runs	Wkts	Av	5wI	10wM
82197	30116	1250	24.09	58	12
18906	*11899*	*486*	*24.48*	*16*	*3*

Best Performances
133 v. Essex at Chelmsford, 1983
*50 v. Kent at Lord's, 1984, and 50 v. Lancashire
   at Blackpool, 1988*
8-40 v. Hampshire at Lord's, 1993
5-23 v. Somerset at Taunton, 1991

John Emburey had to wait too long for a regular first-team spot and perhaps this was one reason why he always seemed such a careful cricketer, unwilling to take too many risks as he tried to wheedle out the opposing batter.

Emburey was usually seen as a specialist bowler, yet over 9,000 runs and 7 centuries suggest, correctly, that despite an eccentric and wayward technique here was run-getting ability. Almost without anyone noticing he made 368 catches, and the six players who beat this total all played more matches. Six times Emburey exceeded 500 runs and 50 wickets in a season, an excellent performance given Test calls and a reduced fixture list and he is one of only 5 players to score 5,000 runs and take 1,000 wickets for Middlesex.

It is, however, as an orthodox off-spin bowler, and worthy successor to Titmus, that Emburey is remembered. His methods perhaps made it difficult for him to 'clean up', since even when at his peak there seemed to be a lack of subtlety and enterprise in his bowling.

He still did very well for Middlesex but it is significant that at Test level his bowling became less and less penetrative the older and more experienced he was. Yet who could possibly fault his second innings 8 for 40, and match figures of 12 for 115 in 68.1 overs as he took full advantage of helpful conditions against Hampshire at Lord's in 1993? To suggest that for a bowler of such ability this should have happened more often may well be deemed churlish. In 64 Tests Emburey took 147 wickets at 38.40. It should have been more for less but the selectors presumably felt he was doing a job. Emburey eventually left Middlesex to be coach at Northampton, where he also played from time to time but with meagre success. Lately Emburey has been cricket manager for the county and in 2002 supervised their gaining of promotion to the First division.

Norman George Featherstone

RHB, OB, 1968-1979

Born: 20 August 1949, Que Que, S. Rhodesia (Zimbabwe)

Batting

M	I	NO	Runs	Av
216	344	34	8882	28.65
193	*176*	*11*	*3423*	*20.74*

50	100	ct/st		
54	8	185		
16	*-*	*56*		

Bowling

Balls	Runs	Wkts	Av	5wI	10wM
7291	3477	137	25.37	3	-
2055	*1493*	*59*	*25.30*	*-*	*-*

Best Performances

147 v. Yorkshire at Scarborough, 1975
82* v. Nottinghamshire at Lord's, 1976
5-32 v. Nottinghamshire at Trent Bridge, 1978
4-10 v. Worcestershire at Worcester, 1978

'Smokey' Featherstone toured England with the South African schools team in 1967 enjoying all-round success. He almost immediately began qualifying for Middlesex and after representing Transvaal B in the Currie Cup made his Middlesex debut against Oxford at the Parks in 1968. After a quiet first season in 1969 Featherstone exceeded 1,000 runs in 1970, and in 1971 he was capped.

Featherstone also exceeded 1,000 runs in 1975, when a total of 1,156 secured an average of 35.03. In 1971 came the first of his eight centuries – an aggressive 120* against Gloucestershire at Tuffley Park, when he and Parfitt added 214 for the fifth wicket after an early collapse. Featherstone played his part in a 5-wicket win with quick runs in the second innings and such a performance was symptomatic of his county career. His next century, against Sussex at Lord's in 1974 was scored as an opener. He dominated a second-wicket stand of 164 with Brearley to put his side into a winning position which his bowlers failed to capitalise on. In the same season, a century in

85 minutes against Yorkshire set up an easy win. Smokey seemed to appreciate the Yorkshire bowling since in the following season at Scarborough he scored 147, the best of his career, and 61 to inspire another fine win. A sixth-wicket stand of 166 between Featherstone and Larry Gomes produced the most aggressive and stylish batting of the match. Two years earlier, Featherstone had given evidence of his ability to produce the goods when needed; a 5th-wicket stand of 200 with John Murray had shown by far the best batting of the match and laid the foundations for victory.

Featherstone's bowling was strangely underused in the first-class game. His best figures came as late as 1978, a second-innings spell of 5 for 38 against Notts. at Trent Bridge confirming him as an unappreciated match-winner.

Featherstone's keen fielding added to his value in limited-overs cricket, and he well merited a successful benefit in 1979. He saw out his career with Glamorgan; a final first-class tally of 13,922 runs (29.37), 277 catches and 181 wickets (27.54) established his value yet somehow he should have done better.

Francis Gilbertson Justice Ford
LHB, SLA, 1886-1899

Born: 14 December 1866, Paddington, London

Died: 7 February 1940, Burwash, Sussex

Batting

M	I	NO	Runs	Av
102	168	7	4650	28.88

50	100	ct/st		
19	10	72		

Bowling

Balls	Runs	Wkts	Av	5wI	10wM
4384	2191	87	25.18	2	-

Best Performances
160 v. Sussex at Lord's, 1899
6-56 v. Lancashire at Lord's, 1899

Francis Ford was a tall, hard-driving left-hander (whose build put contemporaries in mind of a stork) and an accurate bowler who used his height to good effect. He was the best of a well-known cricketing family. Two of his brothers played for Middlesex, a nephew played for Middlesex and Derbyshire, and his great-nephew, John Barclay, skippered Sussex and has written about cricket.

Ford initially made a name at Cambridge where he won his Blue from 1886 to 1889 and captained them in his last season. In 1894/95 he played in all five Tests in Australia but 168 runs (av. 18.66) and 1 wicket must be rated as disappointing for a player who was certainly well worth a trial.

For his county, despite limited appearances, Ford often did very well. His best season, and the only one when he exceeded 1,000 runs, was the penultimate one, when he scored 1,055 runs, average 40.57. Ford enjoyed a particularly fine August when he scored 3 centuries, the last a brilliant 135 in 105 minutes out of 183 against Kent at Lord's. Ford continued in fine form in 1899, with three further centuries. The last was a career best 158 against Gloucestershire at Clifton. He and Warner added 129 for the fifth wicket in 85 minutes, and Ford batted in total for 170 minutes. These were nothing however, compared with his 112 against the 1897 Philadelphians, when according to reports he reached three figures in 55 minutes, the fastest hundred ever for Middlesex, and at Lord's. Eighteen days earlier Ford had scored 150 in 145 minutes against Gloucestershire at Lord's, going in and reaching his century on the third morning.

Francis Ford gave up county cricket aged thirty to earn a living outside the game. His record of 7,359 runs (av. 27.05) and 200 wickets in all first-class cricket does little justice to one whose batting, at its best, was as devastating as any contemporary. Perhaps Francis Ford was an unwitting victim of the accepted class system in cricket at the time.

Angus Robert Charles Fraser

RHB, RFM, 1984-2002

Born: 8 August 1965, Billinge, Lancs.

Batting

M	I	NO	Runs	Av
227	261	64	2431	12.34
294	128	65	724	11.49
50	100	ct/st		
2	-	40		
-	-	51		

Bowling

Balls	Runs	Wkts	Av	5wl	10wM
41425	17934	681	26.33	22	3
14720	8975	345	26.01	8	-

Best Performances

92 v. Surrey at The Oval, 1990
33 v. Essex at Chelmsford, 1997
7-40 v. Leicestershire at Lord's, 1993
5-32 v. Derbyshire at Lord's, 1995

Gus Fraser's career was notable for high quality, accurate and persistent bowling with results which would have been even more impressive were it not for chronic pelvic troubles.

Not until 1987 did he play with any degree of regularity and even then his figures suggested steadiness above all else. However, in 1988, Fraser suddenly forced his way to the front with a season's tally of 80 wickets, average 19.37. Given the new ball he suddenly seemed to gain in pace and accuracy, and the ability to move the ball, and an even better return in 1989 (82 wickets, av. 17.97), saw him make an impressive Test debut. Unfortunately, his pelvic injury emerged in 1990 and although Fraser remained a top-class bowler things were never really the same again. Injury took him out for most of 1991 and he suffered a grim time in 1992. Happily, he recovered to remain a valued bowler, albeit latterly seemingly more intent on bowling maidens than taking wickets.

Fraser's best innings figures came against Leicestershire at Lord's in 1993, with 7 for 40 in 17 overs. He alone of the quick bowlers on view was able to gain much from the wicket, which was doubly welcome since it marked a return to form after a poor spell. Previously his best return had been 7 for 77 against Kent in 1989 and his early career was strewn with excellent performances.

As a batsman, Fraser was usually of little account but had one glory day at The Oval in 1990 when his quickfire 92 included 5 sixes in 12 balls from Neil Kendrick's spinners. In 2001 Fraser, as county captain, narrowly failed to gain promotion and after starting 2002 in the side he retired to become cricket correspondent for the *Independent*. Early evidence suggests he will be an asset to his new profession.

Fraser was invaluable in the limited-overs competitions, with nearly 400 wickets, while a Test record of 177 wickets, average 27.32, suggests true international quality – with better luck it would have been even more impressive.

Robert Alec Gale
LHB, RALB, 1956-1965

Born: 10 December 1933, Old Warden, Bedfordshire

Batting

M	I	NO	Runs	Av
219	398	12	11234	29.10
9	9	0	204	22.66

50	100	ct/st
56	13	108
2	-	2

Bowling

Balls	Runs	Wkts	Av	5wI	10wM
2724	1525	46	33.15	-	-

Best Performances
200 v. Glamorgan at Newport, 1962
86 v. Buckinghamshire at Lord's, 1985
4-57 v. Cambridge University at Fenner's, 1959

At Bedford Modern, the tall and strongly built Bob Gale was said to have shown signs of being overcoached but he showed himself to be a player of promise for Middlesex with some breezy batting in 1956. In 1957, he was elevated to opener where he established himself despite interspersing periods of good form with longer spells when he did little. He improved steadily, albeit unspectacularly and despite some eye trouble which caused him to wear spectacles after 1959, he remained a stalwart until, still under thirty, and with possibly his best years ahead, he began to ease himself out of the county side in order to concentrate on his stockbroking interests.

Despite a satisfactory final career record, the feeling persisted that Gale had never quite possessed the certainty to really fulfil the original promise. A total of 13 centuries is disappointingly meagre for an opener with over 11,000 runs and an average of nearly 30. Only twice did he exceed 140, and the second of these saw his only double century, exactly 200 in 5 hours against Glamorgan in 1962. It should have been the forerunner of several such innings, yet from then on he began to fade from the scene.

Throughout his career, Bob Gale often seemed to be holding something back. That this was not always the case however was shown in his 106 against Kent at Gravesend in 1959. He reached his hundred in 87 minutes and scored all his runs before lunch on the third morning, when Middlesex scored 216 for 2. This superb show of aggression set them up for a deserved victory with 2 minutes of extra time remaining.

Bob Gale's best season – 1,933 runs, average 37.90 – came in 1962, his last full season. It was the 6th time he had recorded four figures, and it certainly should have been more. For much of his county career, Gale's opening partner was Eric Russell. For an established opening pair they were involved in few large stands, the best being 188 against Kent in 1959, when they had to lose their inhibitions in the quest for fast runs. Earlier, in 1957, Gale had helped add 209 for the first wicket with Jack Robertson during Gale's maiden hundred, against Sussex at Lord's.

Bob Gale retains an active role in Middlesex cricket and in 2002, he became president.

RHB, RM, 1975-1998

Born: 6 June 1957, Kingsbury

Batting

M	I	NO	Runs	Av
412	631	93	28411	52.80
433	398	61	11742	34.84
50	**100**	**ct/st**		
137	77	393		
73	11	147		

Bowling

Balls	Runs	Wkts	Av	5wI	10wM
7756	3650	129	28.29	2	-
5582	4313	150	28.75	4	-

Best Performances

258 v. Somerset at Bath, 1984
143 v. Sussex at Hove, 1985*
5-34 v. Glamorgan at Swansea, 1982
4-30 v. Gloucestershire at Bristol, 1989

Mike Gatting was a square-built pugnacious-looking individual who regularly slaughtered attacks from all classes of the game in the sort of way that persuaded the opposition that they were no longer keen on bowling.

Gatting's record for Middlesex was superb. His career totals of runs and centuries, half-centuries (214) and 1,000 runs in a season (17) are beaten only by Hendren, while Gatting is the first batsman in the history of Middlesex cricket to enjoy a career average of over 50. Gatting scored 8 double centuries for his county, a figure beaten only by 'the twins' Hendren and J.W. Hearne. Gatting's best score was a magnificent 258 against Somerset at Bath in 1984. Scored on the first day of the match, the innings included 8 sixes and was at the time the county's highest innings for 35 years. It is still the 7th highest innings ever for Middlesex. Then, as late as 1998 Gatting, opening with Langer against Essex, played an epic 241 in 520 minutes, with 8 sixes. This is the best-ever score at the Walkers' ground. Along the way, he and Langer added 372 together, the record for the Middlesex first wicket. Gatting had proved his high-scoring

abilities in 1983 – his savage 216 in 241 minutes against the New Zealanders remains the best score for Middlesex against any touring team, while the third-wicket stand of 318 with Radley remains the best for any wicket against tourists. Even higher had been the 338 added for the same wicket by Gatting and Brearley against Derbyshire at Derby in 1981 – Gatting's share was an unbeaten 186 – while in 1993 Gatting (182) and Ramprakash put on 321 for the same wicket against Yorkshire at Scarborough. Gatting enjoyed big stands; when scoring his 210 against Nottinghamshire at Lord's in 1988 he and Keith Brown added 264 in 63 overs. Down the card, against Northamptonshire at Lord's in 1976, Gatting the tyro played second fiddle to Phil Edmonds as they added 160 for the seventh wicket.

Surprisingly, Gatting only once scored a hundred in each innings, following 117 with a ferocious 163* in 169 balls, with 6 sixes, against Warwickshire at Coventry in 1992. Only one colleague reached 50 yet Middlesex won by 226 runs in a genuine one-man effort.

Gatting exceeded 1,000 runs in a season 17 times, and 3 times went on to 2,000, with a best of 2,150, average 71.66 in 1984. He scored 2,057 runs in 1991 and exactly 2,000 in 1992.

Early in his career, Gatting was rated highly as a medium fast bowler. Against Glamorgan at Swansea in 1982, he helped run through the opposition on the first day with five for 34 in 12 overs but as time went by he understandably bowled less. Gatting's build did not suggest fleetness in the field but his safe hands pouched 393 catches to place him 4th on the county's all-time list.

Gatting was a generally successful Middlesex skipper from 1983 until late May 1997, when he stepped down in favour of Ramprakash because he felt it was the thing to do. Such a changeover compared most favourably with the regular bloody coups at other counties. Unfortunately, his subsequent short spell as Middlesex manager was not a success.

Gatting retired with a batting career record of 36,549 runs, average 49.52, with 94 centuries. His sometimes disappointing Test career saw him finish with 4,409 runs, av. 35.55. He often skippered the side well but he tended to wear his heart on his sleeve and was also unlucky. Sadly, Australia 1994/95 as a player was a tour too many.

The belligerence and power of Gatting is captured in this superb action photograph.

Laurence Herbert Gray

RHB, RFM, 1934-1951

Born: 16 December 1915, Tottenham
Died: 3 January 1983, Langdon Hills, Essex

Batting

M	I	NO	Runs	Av
204	233	119	772	6.77
50	100	ct/st		
-	-	119		

Bowling

Balls	Runs	Wkts	Av	5wI	10wM
34582	14485	600	24.14	26	3

Best Performances

32 v. Cambridge University at Fenner's, 1946
8-59 v. Kent at Maidstone, 1938

Laurie Gray, tall with long arms and legs, first made his mark in London schools cricket, being too fast for the ease of mind of some parents. In the county game he was more of a 'bread and butter' bowler, but he may possibly have reached the highest class had the Second World War not robbed him of a number of good years. On the resumption of county cricket in 1946, Gray was manifestly at his peak, maintaining a good speed without making his pre-war mistake of pitching too short too often. However, after 1947, an arthritic hip reduced his effectiveness and he gradually played less frequently. Gray, capped in 1937 and a successful beneficiary in 1948, enjoyed a consistent and generally hard-working county career interspersed with a number of excellent performances. Statistically his 8 for 59 against Kent at Maidstone in 1938 was his best effort. He scythed through the star-studded Kent batting to such effect that they were all out on the first afternoon but unfortunately, Gray's own batting colleagues collapsed twice and the match was over, with Middlesex defeated, late on the second day.

Another magnificent effort, in 1946, when he attained match figures of 11 for 34 in 35.5 overs against Hampshire at Lord's brought better luck, Middlesex earning a resounding win. Weeks later, Gray was extracting unusual life from the Trent Bridge featherbed as first innings figures of 7 for 85 and a match total of 10 for 114 saw to it that his side were victorious by an innings. Gray enjoyed his greatest success in this 1946 season, taking 95 wickets, average 16.90 for the county, and 102 in all matches. In 1947, he again played his part. His best innings figures were 7 for 69 during the win over Glamorgan and he overcame the handicap of a lack of regular pace support with 92 wickets (22.46).

Gray's career from then was one of gentle decline. The heart and lungs were still in good order, but the unflinching efforts now took their toll on his legs and, especially his hips. After retirement, Gray spent 17 years on the first-class umpires' list, officiating in four Test matches and only ill health enforced his premature departure. He had been an embellishment to the professional game.

Walter Henry Hadow
RHB, RA slow, 1870-1879

Born: 25 September 1849, Marylebone
Died: 15 September 1898, Dupplin Castle, Perthshire

Batting

M	I	NO	Runs	Av
37	67	4	1436	22.79

50	100	ct/st
4	2	44

Bowling

Balls	Runs	Wkts	Av	5wI	10wM
4134	1462	103	14.19	9	3

Best Performances
217 v. MCC at Lord's, 1871
8-35 v. Nottinghamshire at Trent Bridge, 1874

W.H. Hadow was one of four brothers who all played for Middlesex in the great days of the amateur cricketer, and he was most certainly the best.

A brilliant schoolboy cricketer who was allegedly scoring centuries at a very early age, Hadow was a powerful, wristy batsman, 6ft in height and a slow round-arm bowler whose powers of spin and flight occasionally played havoc with the best of batsmen.

Hadow gained his Blue at Oxford without achieving a great deal but really established his reputation when scoring a brilliant double century against MCC at Lord's in 1871. Aged twenty-one, he remained the youngest scorer of a double century for the county for 40 years, and it was the first double for Middlesex, the first at Lord's for more than 50 years, and his own maiden first-class century. He hit 4 fives and 16 fours, batted 5 hours and 30 minutes and his 217 came out of 365 runs scored while he was at the wicket. In all respects it was a stupendous innings and no reflection on Hadow that everything he subsequently achieved was perhaps an anticlimax.

Hadow scored one other century for the county, 140 in over 4 hours against the powerful Nottinghamshire attack in 1878, but he was probably already being affected by the health problems which caused his early death. After a few more games he dropped out of the side when still under thirty years old.

Hadow was also a superb bowler. His best match was against Nottinghamshire at Trent Bridge in 1874 when he followed 4 for 9 in the first innings with 8 for 33 in the second, yet Middlesex still lost. Hadow also had match figures of 11 for 107 against Notts. at Prince's in 1875 and followed with 12 for 120 against Yorkshire at Sheffield in the following match. In this season, Hadow had a run of 34 wickets for 359 in 6 consecutive innings. It was sad indeed that such genius was so soon stifled.

Interestingly, of the four Hadow brothers who played for Middlesex, W.H., A.A. and E.M. all died young, whereas P.F., a fine tennis and billiards player, lived into his nineties.

Nigel Esme Haig

RHB, RFM, 1912-1934

Born: 12 December 1887, Kensington, London
Died: 27 October 1966, Eastbourne, Sussex

Batting

M	I	NO	Runs	Av
417	630	39	12289	20.79
50	100	ct/st		
49	11	182		

Bowling

Balls	Runs	Wkts	Av	5wI	10wM
64239	24264	931	26.06	41	2

Best Performances
131 v. Sussex at Lord's, 1920
7-33 v. Kent at Canterbury, 1920

Nigel Haig was a talented and tireless all-rounder described elsewhere as seemingly made of whipcord. He also captained the county from 1929 to 1934, not the most successful period for Middlesex but Haig at least gave his all and expected the same from those under his command. He was an aggressive batsman with a good eye and despite a tendency to play fast bowlers from somewhere adjacent to the square-leg umpire, he scored runs aplenty and usually at a good pace. As a bowler, at slightly above medium pace he had an awkward action with unusually jerky body movements but swung the ball more than expected and could plug away for long spells.

Haig, an Etonian who suprisingly failed to get into the XI there, exceeded 1,000 runs in a season on two occasions and also took 100 wickets twice. In 1929, he achieved both feats to become the first and only amateur to perform the season's 'double' of 1,000 runs and 100 wickets for the county. This was a pretty triumphant first season as skipper for Haig. The county finished sixth (under his leader-ship it was their best performance) and his 1,228 runs (av. 25.58) and 106 wickets (av. 22.53) were both season's bests.

Haig, whose 417 appearances were by far a record for a Middlesex amateur, scored 11 centuries. His best was his first, a brilliant 131 in 110 minutes against Sussex at Lord's in 1920. Haig dominated a third-wicket stand of 227 with J.W. Hearne in an amazing innings which saw the first four batsmen hit centuries. Later in the season when Middlesex – who finally won the title – won a vital five-run victory over Kent at Canterbury, Haig achieved his best-ever innings bowling figures of 7 for 33 and in fact took all his wickets in 37 balls.

Finally, Nigel Haig, an all-round sportsman who excelled at real and lawn tennis, very nearly became unique. His uncle, Lord Harris, was consulted when economic necessities forced Haig to consider turning professional. Perhaps it was a pity Haig, an old Etonian, and nephew of one of the most reactionary of Lords at Lord's, decided against this worthy profession.

George Edmead Hart
RHB, RM, 1926-1939

Born: 13 January 1902, Harlington
Died: 11 April 1987 Barnstaple, Devon

Batting

M	I	NO	Runs	Av
194	304	31	5711	20.91

50	100	ct/st		
23	4	58		

Bowling

Balls	Runs	Wkts	Av	5wl	10wM
2190	1082	21	51.52	-	-

Best Performances
121 v. Hampshire at Lord's, 1934
3-64 v. Gloucestershire at Lord's, 1928

George Hart, the type of paid player that was once the backbone of the County Championship, was also in some respect one of the more unlucky of the Middlesex professionals in that almost throughout his career there were amateurs (some of whom were good enough, but not all) or rising young professionals to take his place. At times Hart seemed almost permanently 12th man. It was probably due to his never being sure of a secure place that his batting, with its stylish off drive, did not develop in the hoped-for manner, though he did become one of the best and most versatile fieldsmen.

Hart did enough to win his county cap in 1929 and in 1939 was awarded a joint benefit with Joe Hulme, another who had similar misfortunes.

Despite appearing in 194 matches, Hart never really had a full season. He was at his best in 1934 when with 976 runs (av. 24.40) he came nearer to 1,000 runs than in any other season. Even here, Hart was unfortunate, since a broken hand sustained from a blow from Derbyshire fast bowler Bill Copson kept him out of the last few matches.

Early in the season, Hart obtained his maiden first-class century, opening the batting against Hants at Lord's. He reached three figures in 210 minutes and his final 121, which remained his best score, contained 10 fours. In the following match, Hart scored 80 and 107 against Sussex but he never really showed such impressive run-scoring again, although he did have the occasional 'flurry'. For instance in 1937, having missed a number of games, he scored 84 of a 2nd-wicket stand of 211 with Bill Edrich against Somerset at Lord's and Hart, scoring 118, dominated a 2nd-wicket stand of 150 with the same player in the following game against Kent at headquarters. All four of his centuries were scored at Lord's and although never really consistent he seemed happier there than on his travels. A great 'nearly' man was George Hart, deservedly well-liked by both his fellow players and supporters.

After retirement, Hart became coach at Shrewsbury school and did some Minor Counties umpiring.

Herbert Bailey Hayman

RHB, 1893-1901

Born: 5 October 1873, Hendon
Died: 31 July 1930, Winslow, Bucks.

Batting

M	I	NO	Runs	Av
86	154	11	3593	25.12
50	**100**	**ct/st**		
19	3	37		

Bowling

Balls	Runs	Wkts	Av	5wI	10wM
149	75	2	37.50	-	-

Best Performances

152 v. Yorkshire at Lord's, 1896
2-9 v. Yorkshire at Lord's, 1901

Herbert Hayman was a steady and fairly orthodox batsman who scored heavily for Hampstead Cricket Club for a number of years and who promised much for Middlesex prior to his premature retirement while still in his twenties.

During his short county career Hayman scored runs regularly and his first century, which was to remain his best score for the county, came when he was aged twenty-two against Yorkshire at Lord's in 1896. Hayman scored 152 and added 218 for the first wicket with A.E. Stoddart. Contemporary reports suggested that he was a batsman headed for the top but for whatever reason it was not to be, though he did score two more hundreds for the county. His 104* against Kent at Catford in 1898 was a specially fine knock since he

carried his bat out of 213 and no other Middlesex player in the whole match reached 30. Hayman's other hundred came in 1901, his last season. He scored 110 in 85 minutes against Gloucestershire at Lord's and he and P.F. Warner added 200 for the first wicket at more than two runs a minute. It was brilliant stuff but sadly Gloucestershire were able to play out time on the final afternoon. Against Sussex at Lord's in July 1901, Hayman scored a bright 58, and added 94 for the first wicket with Warner. That innings terminated his first-class county career, a career which had promised so much but never really seemed to take off as expected.

There was to be much high scoring for Hampstead. He scored 164 in 95 minutes out of 273-2 against Eltham in 1901, and in 1905 for Hampstead against Upper Tooting, he was run out for 201 in 80 minutes hitting 3 sixes and 30 fours. At this time Hayman would normally have been at his peak as a county batsman, yet his first-class career was by now long finished.

Desmond Leo Haynes
RHB, 1989-1994

Born: 15 February 1956, St James, Barbados

Batting

M	I	NO	Runs	Av
95	162	18	7071	49.10
97	95	10	4056	47.71

50	100	ct/st
31	21	48
34	6	32

Bowling

Balls	Runs	Wkts	Av	5wI	10wM
310	192	4	48.00	-	-
630	463	7	66.14	-	-

Best Performances
255* v. Sussex at Lord's, 1990
149 v. Lancashire at Old Trafford, 1990*

Signed as an opening batsman replacement in the wake of the tragic death of Wilf Slack, Haynes took to county cricket as if to the manner born. When Haynes signed for Middlesex he had to some extent been batting under the massive Test shadows of Richards and Greenidge but 7,487 runs, average 42.49, confirm that here too was a fine Test batsman.

Haynes exceeded 1,000 runs in his first season with 1,446 runs, average 45.18, the best of his three hundreds being a superb 206* against Kent at Uxbridge when he added 361 for the first wicket with Ian Hutchinson. In the following game, also at Uxbridge, Haynes scored 143* while putting together 319 for the second wicket with Gatting. Haynes' good form continued with a vengeance in 1990 when he amassed 2,346 runs, average 69.00, the best total for 39 years. He hit 8 centuries, including a memorable first day 255* in 353 balls, with a century before lunch, against Sussex at Lord's and an only slightly less trouble-free unbeaten 220 against

Essex, when he and Roseberry put on 306 for the first wicket. Haynes also scored a hundred before lunch against Yorkshire at Headingley in the same season, and the same pair added 266 against Nottinghamshire at Trent Bridge in 1992. Haynes also scored 1,513 runs in this season.

Desmond Haynes was only able to give Middlesex five seasons, and 95 matches, so his career total of 7,071 runs is particularly noteworthy. His career average of 49.10 put him in 5th position among regular Middlesex batsmen. Rarely did he seem to bat with less than complete authority and assurance and his mastery must have served as an inspirational example to other Middlesex batsmen.

Haynes, who was involved in West Indies first-wicket record Test partnerships of 298 and 296 with Gordon Greenidge, finally retired in 1996 with 26,030 runs, average 45.90, with 61 centuries – fitting figures for one very little below the really great.

John Thomas Hearne

RHB, RM, 1888-1923

Born: 3 May 1867, Chalfont St Giles, Bucks.
Died: 17 April 1944, Chalfont St Giles, Bucks.

Batting

M	I	NO	Runs	Av
453	630	223	4598	11.29
50	100	ct/st		
4	-	310		

Bowling

Balls	Runs	Wkts	Av	5wI	10wM
104260	38167	2093	18.23	171	30

Best Performances

56* v. Essex at Leyton, 1905, and v. Essex at
   Leyton, 1906
9-32 v. Nottinghamshire at Trent Bridge, 1891

Jack T. Hearne (the initial is to distinguish him from his junior namesake, Jack W. Hearne) took a fairly long, bounding run up to the wicket and with a high and very easy action delivered outswingers, inswingers, off-cutters, all at a pace which varied between slow medium and fast medium on a length which rarely varied at all. His was a style for long spells and economy, and in twelve of his seasons he bowled more than 6,000 balls. His accuracy and penetration is illustrated by the fact that in ten seasons he took 100 or more wickets for Middlesex, and 15 times he exceeded the 100 in all first-class matches.

Hearne was certainly a wicket-taker. Second only to Titmus in his total of Middlesex wickets, he obtained them for an average of less than one every 50 balls. A remarkable 35 times he took 7 or more wickets in an innings while he took 10 or more in a match 30 times. Both are Middlesex records by a fair distance. Hearne's best innings fig-

ures were 9 for 32 against Nottinghamshire at Trent Bridge in 1891. Hearne bowled 40.5 overs and in a rain-ruined match took 8 of his wickets before lunch on the third day. Hearne also took 9 for 68 against Lancashire at Old Trafford in 1898 and 9 for 78 in 1908 against Yorkshire at Bradford. Curiously his best figures for the county at Lord's were 'only' 8 for 22 against Lancs in 1891, when at one point he took 4 wickets with 6 balls and actually had match figures of 11 for 47. Hearne's best match figures came in 1898, again v. Lancashire but at Old Trafford. To the first innings 9 for 68 mentioned above he added 7 for 46. Despite this 16 for 114, he finished on the losing side. Hearne had also finished with the losers when taking 14 for 65 gainst Yorkshire. Thankfully, when Hearne took 15 for 154 against Notts at Trent Bridge in 1893, Middlesex won. Hearne achieved three 'hat-tricks' for Middlesex and against Essex at Lord's in 1902 went on to take 4 wickets with 5 balls.

Hearne's best season was 1893, when he took 145 wickets for Middlesex (av. 16.23); 17 times he took 5 or more wickets in an innings (still a joint record) and taking 10 or more in a match 5 times was also a record at the time.

Hearne played in 12 Tests for England. Although without startling success, he did achieve a hat-trick against Australia in 1899. He also made many first-class appearances for MCC. His first-class record for all teams was an impressive 7,205 runs (av. 11.98), 426 catches, 3,061 wickets (av. 17.75). Three times he took more than 200 first-class wickets in a season – 257 (av. 14.28) in 1896 being his best. While not noted as a batsman, he did help Tom Hayward put on 156 for the ninth wicket for Players v. Gentlemen at Lord's in 1896. Hearne's share was 71 and it remained a Lord's best for that wicket until 1920. Hearne's first-class career stretched from 1888 to 1923, 36 seasons, a Middlesex record, albeit with gaps late on. His final match was against Scotland, at the age of 56 years and 90 days. He remains the second oldest player for the county.

He was of course a member of cricket's most extended family, 13 having played first-class cricket, 6 in Test matches. His brothers Walter and Herbert played for Kent. J.W. Hearne was a first cousin, albeit twice removed, J.T. was Thomas Hearne's first cousin once removed. J.T. Hearne's great-nephew was South African lawn-tennis star Eric Sturgess.

Above: John with his wife Edith Anna.

Right: The bowling action of John Thomas Hearne.

John William Hearne

RHB, LBG, 1909-1936

Born: 11 February 1891, Hillingdon
Died: 14 September 1965, West Drayton

Batting

M	I	NO	Runs	Av
465	744	73	27612	41.15
50	100	ct/st		
115	71	240		

Bowling

Balls	Runs	Wkts	Av	5wI	10wM
72082	33291	1438	23.15	88	17

Best Performances

285* v. Essex at Leyton, 1929
9-61 v. Derbyshire at Chesterfield, 1933

Jack W. Hearne's career overlapped that of his senior namesake by a few seasons. He joined the Lord's staff aged fifteen and stayed until his retirement from the position of chief coach. 'Young Jack', slightly built, almost fragile looking, was a batsman who relied more on timing than power (though employing a strong drive), and a leg spinner relying on subtlety and flight rather than power of spin.

'Young Jack' made a marvellous start to his career, completing the 1,000 run/100 wicket 'double' in all first-class matches when aged twenty in 1911. Two seasons later, Hearne completed the 'double' for Middlesex alone, in 21 matches scoring 1,663 runs (51.97) and taking 107 wickets (22.04). He went on to repeat the feat for his county in 1920 (1,638 runs, av. 54.60, 123 wickets, av. 18.22 in 22 matches) and 1923 (1,252 runs, av. 46.37, 103 wickets, av. 19.48 in 21 matches). Eventually, he became the only Middlesex all-rounder to exceed 20,000 runs and 1,000 wickets in a county career.

As a batsman, only Hendren and Gatting have exceeded his 71 centuries for the county, while Hendren alone beat Hearne's

11 double centuries, the highest of which was a monumental 285* against Essex at Leyton in 1929. It was at the time the highest innings for Middlesex and, at nearly eight and a half hours, the longest. Perhaps Hearne's most noteworthy innings, however, was his 234* against Somerset at Lord's in 1911. In an innings marked by firm driving, he was at the wickets for 325 minutes and hit 30 fours. He was only 20 years and 152 days old and remains the youngest scorer of a double century for Middlesex. In 1931, Hearne scored a hundred in each innings against Glamorgan at Lord's and in the same season, opening the batting, his carried his bat for 152 out of 309 against Leicestershire at Leicester. Though normally regarded as one of the 'steady' school, Hearne also scored more than 100 runs before lunch on three occasions. The most notable of these was against Hampshire at Lord's in 1919 when on the extended second morning, when he took his score from 53 to 171, Hendren went from 62 to 201 and the 325 they added in under 3 hours remains a fourth-wicket record for the county.

In exceeding 1,000 runs in 16 seasons, Hearne is second only to Hendren. His best was 2,021 runs (av. 74.85) in 1914 when he was a mere twenty-three years old. Hearne still shares two partnership records for the county, the fourth wicket mentioned above, and the second, 380 with Frank Tarrant against Lancashire at Lord's in 1914, then the county's highest for any wicket. Until finally beaten in 1948, the nearest approach was by Hearne and Hendren – 375 for the third wicket against Hampshire in 1923.

As a bowler, Hearne is third on the list of Middlesex wicket-takers. His best analysis was 9 for 61 in a 2-hour spell against Derbyshire at Chesterfield in 1933. He also had 9 for 82 against Surrey at Lord's in 1911 – a match-winning effort when aged twenty. His best match bowling was 14 for 146 against Essex in 1914. Hearne performed the 'hat-trick' against Essex at Lord's in 1911, repeating it against the same opposition at Leyton in 1922. He performed the 'match double' (100 runs and 10 wickets) a remarkable 6 times, more than any other player for any county in the championship.

'Young Jack's' record for 24 Tests – 806 runs (26.00) and 30 wickets (48.73) – was somewhat mediocre and perhaps this was partly due to uncertain health, yet by and large there is little doubt that he was the best of the cricketing Hearnes.

Above: John William (left) with his father.

Right: John William demonstrating his bowling action.

Thomas Hearne

RHB, RM roundarm, 1859-1875

Born: 4 September 1826, Chalfont St Peter, Bucks.
Died: 13 May 1900, Ealing

Batting

M	I	NO	Runs	Av
59	96	5	1799	19.76
50	100	ct/st		
5	2	53/2		

Bowling

Balls	Runs	Wkts	Av	5wI	10wM
18112	2835	209	14.10	12	2

Best Performances

146 v. Surrey at Islington, 1866
6-12 v. Surrey at Lord's, 1869

'Old Tom', as he was known to distinguish him from his groundsman son, 'Young Tom', was the first of the Hearnes to distinguish himself at cricket. He was a hard and punishing hitter, always seeking to score quickly especially from drives, a steady medium-paced round-arm bowler, an adept long stop and a remarkably fine fielder anywhere else.

He first came to public notice as a member of the United All-England XI. In 1859, he had shared in an opening stand of 149 for this XI with Robert Carpenter, for these times a very high partnership. Hearne also distinguished himself for the Players, scoring 122 against the Gentlemen at Lord's in 1866. From 1857 to 1876, he played for MCC and in 1861/62, he toured Australia with H.H. Stephenson's team.

All this time Hearne was a stalwart professional for Middlesex. In 1864 he became the first Middlesex professional to score a century – 125 against MCC at Islington. Two seasons later, against Surrey at Islington, Hearne compiled his best first-class score, 146, and added 161 with his skipper V.E. Walker, a county sixth-wicket record at the time.

Hearne's best bowling analysis came in Middlesex's first game at Lord's against Surrey in 1869. 10.2 overs, 7 maidens, 6 for 12 were his first innings figures as he and George Howitt skittled Surrey for 37. Against Nottinghamshire at Trent Bridge in 1866, Hearne had match figures of 12 for 76 as he and R.D. Walker bowled unchanged to outplay Nottinghamshire. A year before, Hearne (10-84) and A.J.A. Wilkinson had bowled unchanged to thrash Hampshire by an innings. Against Kent at Islington in 1868, Hearne performed the first hat-trick for the county, a feat not repeated for 28 years. This fine all rounder scored more than 5,000 runs and took nearly 300 wickets in first-class cricket.

For many years on the Lord's staff, Hearne eventually became ground superintendent. After a stroke in 1876 curtailed his career as a player, Hearne became secretary of the Cricketers' Fund Friendly Society. He was also a tailor and tobacconist in Ealing. His son George Francis was a useful player who became Lord's pavilion clerk while grandson Thomas John Hearne played for Middlesex.

Elias Henry Hendren
RHB, 1907-1937

Born: 5 February 1889, Turnham Green
Died: 4 October 1962, Tooting Bec, South
London

Batting
M	I	NO	Runs	Av
581	928	119	40302	49.81

50	100	ct/st
190	119	561

Bowling
Balls	Runs	Wkts	Av	5wl	10wM
4019	2065	39	52.94	1	-

Best Performances
301* v. Worcestershire at Dudley, 1933
5-43 v. Nottinghamshire at Trent Bridge, 1919

The son of Irish immigrants named O'Hanrahan, he was Christened Elias but universally known as 'Patsy' or 'Pat', and although never living in Ireland, from the long upper lip to the pixylike appearance, there could have been no doubt whatsoever as to his ancestry.

Hendren, whose brother Dennis was also a cricketer and umpire, first played in 1907 but not until 1919, when he was thirty, did he really make his mark. He made his mark with a vengeance, however, and for nearly twenty years he was among the most regular scorers and attractive cricketers in the game. He was the typical working-class Middlesex cricketer, a genre which no longer seems to exist. Here surely is a reason for the slump in Middlesex and even national cricket. It has lost the working classes.

A straight statistical analysis of Hendren's county career is indeed impressive. He played 571 matches in 27 seasons (only Titmus beats him on both counts) and his tally of 40,302 is way ahead of Gatting in second spot, while Hendren's 119 first-class centuries should remain the county record for all time, likewise his 15 double centuries for the county. Hendren's best score was 301* against

Worcestershire at Dudley in 1933, in 7 hours. Aged 44 years and 169 days, he was the oldest scorer of a triple century ever in the Championship. Equally remarkable was his unbeaten 277 out of 435 against Kent at Lord's in 1922. He was batting over 6 hours, hit 37 fours and cut, hooked and pulled ferociously. Against Surrey at Lord's in 1937 in his final championship match, he hit 103. At 48 years, 206 days he was, and remains, the oldest Middlesex centurion.

Three times Hendren scored a century in each innings for Middlesex and twice, in 1931 and 1933, he made it 3 in 3. In compiling his county record 119 hundreds, he scored at least one every season from 1913 to 1937, and against every other first-class county. Hendren was involved in a particularly outstanding feat in 1919, when before lunch on the second day of the Hampshire game at Lord's he (62 to 201) and Young Jack Hearne both exceeded 100 runs in the session.

Hendren scored more than 1,000 runs in a season twenty times, a Middlesex record (Gatting lies second on 17). His county's season's record of 2,669 runs (av. 83.40) in 1923 remains the best, even despite 1947. Hendren had 2,623 runs (av. 79.48) in 1928, 2,514 (av.

Denis Compton (left) and Hendren walk out to bat against Surrey at
the Oval in 1936.

62.85) in 1933, and beat 2,000 a further four times. He scored 12 centuries in 1928, 11 in 1923. Only Compton (13 in 1947) beats him.

Hendren shares three Middlesex partnership records, namely 325 for the fourth wicket with J.W. Hearne v. Hampshire at Lord's in 1919, 271 unbeaten for the seventh with Frank Mann against Notts at Trent Bridge in 1925 and 160 unbroken with Jack Durston for the nineth against Essex at Leyton in 1927. He also added 314 for the second with Harry Lee against Hampshire at Lord's in 1928, 375 for the third with J.W. Hearne against Hampshire at Southampton in 1923, and 301 with Tim Killick against Sussex at Hove in 1928, also for the third. Then there was the 332 he added with Fred Price for the fifth against Worcestershire at Dudley in 1933.

Pat Hendren's 561 catches represent a Middlesex career record by a long way – yet often he fielded in the outfield. He did little bowling. After retirement Hendren did some coaching and was Middlesex scorer, a job he found hard but performed to the best of his ability.

Hendren's Test record of 3,525 runs (47.63) and his full first-class total of 57,611 runs (50.80) seem of little consequence. Here was the all-time Middlesex hero.

Perceval Jeffery Thornton Henery
RHB, RA round-arm spin, 1879-1894

Born: 6 June 1859, London
Died: 10 August 1938, Old Cleeve, Washford, Somerset

Batting

M	I	NO	Runs	Av
72	114	9	1495	14.23

50	100	ct/st		
5	-	38		

Bowling

Balls	Runs	Wkts	Av	5wI	10wM
531	190	11	17.27	1	-

Best Performances
81* v. Sussex at Hove, 1892
5-56 v. Yorkshire at Lord's, 1880

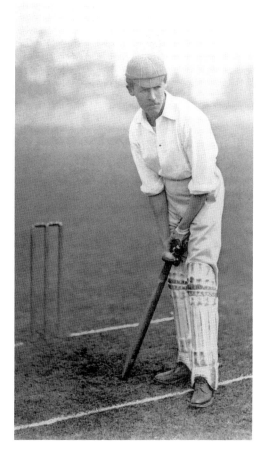

Perceval Henery was in many ways a typical amateur of his time in that he had a fairly lengthy county career yet did not really play many matches.

From the Bayswater area of London, he was a hard-hitting batsman but sometimes rather irresolute, and a slow-medium bowler whose round-arm style relied much on sharp spin rather than flight. Henery had an excellent all-round record at Harrow which unfortunately was never really transferred to the first-class game but he won his Blue at Cambridge in 1882 and 1883 and played for various MCC and Gentlemen's teams and once, in 1883/84, for British Guiana.

Henery scored only one century in first-class cricket, a brilliant 138* for the Gentlemen against Oxford University at Oxford in 1888. Henery batted at number 7, hit 17 fours and the score advanced from 184 for 5 to 447 all out during his innings, which converted seemingly certain defeat to an honourable draw. Unfortunately, such valuable batting efforts were few and far between. Henery's best score for Middlesex was 81 not out in 125 minutes against Sussex at Hove in 1892. Again he ran out of partners as he seemed to be the only batsman prepared to show enterprise on a poor wicket and his batting had much to do with an innings victory.

Surprisingly, Henery took only 11 wickets for Middlesex and 5 of these came in one innings – for 56 runs against Yorkshire at Lord's in 1880, when his victims included three Test players, yet Middlesex finished as the losers by 88 runs. In one of the great mysteries of Middlesex cricket, in another 14 seasons, Henery never took another wicket after that match.

In a first-class career of 94 matches, Henery scored 2,229 runs, average 15.80, took 53 catches and obtained 12 wickets, average 17.41. He remained a real force in minor cricket, once scoring 202* for Hampshire Rovers at Portsmouth in 1891, while he also played cricket in British Guiana, where he had business and family interests, but overall his career must rank as disappointing.

Ronald William Hooker

RHB, RM, 1956-1969

Born: 22 February 1935, Lower Clapton, London

Batting

M	I	NO	Runs	Av
300	442	71	8222	22.16
26	26	9	422	24.82

50	100	ct/st
35	5	301
-	-	14

Bowling

Balls	Runs	Wkts	Av	5wI	10wM
32089	13457	490	27.46	16	-
1246	695	37	18.78	1	-

Best Performances

137 v. Kent at Gravesend, 1959
43 v. Northamptonahire at Lord's, 1963
7-18 v. Worcestershire at Worcester, 1965
6-6 v. Surrey at Lord's, 1969

Ron Hooker was a basically uncomplicated sort of cricketer who liked scoring in boundaries and bowled medium pace, just doing enough to cause care.

When establishing himself in 1959, Hooker was compared with Denis Compton by some commentators – for somewhat elusive reasons – but this hard-working all-rounder gave excellent service. His 1959 season started with 90 in 75 minutes at Oxford and he followed this with a dashing effort against Kent at Gravesend. A remarkable 122 out of his innings of 137 came in boundaries and Hooker did much to put his side into an ultimately winning position on the first day. Hooker scored 1,449 runs (av. 30.18) in 1959 and such form was never really repeated, though he did score 1,083 runs in 1963. As his batting declined however, he became of more value as a bowler. Medium-paced seam was becoming increasingly important with the emergence of limited-overs cricket, and Hooker worked hard at this burgeoning second string to his bow.

His bowling peak was reached in 1965. As the county's leading wicket-taker with 90 wickets (av. 24.86), he three times took 7 wickets in an innings. The best of these was 7 for 18 in 12.3 overs against Worcestershire at Worcester, when he used seaming conditions and a strong crosswind more effectively than faster and ostensibly more accomplished bowlers. Earlier that season, he achieved figures of 7 for 125 against Somerset at Taunton – much less notable bowling against batsmen seeking quick runs and, for the most part, getting them. He put in a far better performance later in the season at Lord's when, taking the new ball against Hampshire, he had figures of 7 for 24 in 22.2 overs as the visitors batted without enterprise in difficult conditions on the opening day.

Hooker's career then went into decline and he played no more after 1969, still only thirty-four, a player remembered and respected but whose actual role had been hard to define. He appeared for Buckinghamshire in the Minor Counties championship, while outside cricket he became involved in the electronics engineering industry.

Joseph Harold Anthony Hulme

RHB, RMF, 1929-1939

Born: 26 August 1904, Stafford
Died: 27 September 1991, Winchmore Hill

Batting

M	I	NO	Runs	Av
223	346	45	8015	26.62

50	100	ct/st
40	12	109

Bowling

Balls	Runs	Wkts	Av	5wI	10wM
6866	3223	89	36.21	-	-

Best Performances

143 v. Gloucestershire at Bristol, 1938
4-44 v. Derbyshire at Derby, 1934

In common with his almost exact contemporary George Hart, Joe Hulme was unlucky in that he rarely had a sufficiently secure place for him to do himself complete justice. He often found himself doing 12th man duties but nevertheless he was a magnificent servant to the county, who gave him his cap in 1930, and a joint benefit with Hart in 1939.

Hulme was a forcing batsman, very fast between the wickets and a seam bowler slightly on the quick side of medium who on occasion was entrusted with the new ball. Most of all, however, Hulme was a magnificent fielder with a great sense of anticipation, speed onto the ball and a good arm. In a more enlightened environment than Middlesex in the thirties, this asset alone could have guaranteed him his place.

Hulme topped 1,000 runs in a season on three occasions, his best tally being 1,258 (av. 34.94) in 1934. He actually scored 4 centuries during the season, including his season's best, 134 against Somerset at Lord's, an innings that included 18 fours and lasted 3 hours. He and Hendren added 106 for the third wicket in only an hour and then Hulme and R.W.V.

Robins put on a quick-fire 117 for the fourth wicket. Three more centuries followed in only a few weeks, including 108 against Glamorgan at Lord's when he and Gubby Allen added 212, a sixth-wicket record for 31 years. It was truly a golden spell for Joe Hulme. In 1936 Hulme also scored four centuries, all unselfish and effective, and he exceeded 1,000 runs for the third and last time; some fine young batsmen were now flexing their muscles. Not that Hulme's day was quite done: though struggling for a regular place he made 1938 notable for his best-ever score, a match-deciding 143 in 185 minutes against Gloucestershire at Bristol, he and Walter Robins adding 116 in 78 minutes for the fifth wicket. Loss of form towards the end suggested, correctly, the writing was on the wall.

Hulme enjoyed great renown as a soccer player for Arsenal and England; he also helped build the legendary Tottenham side of the 1950s.

Rev. Edgar Thomas Killick

RHB, 1926-1939

Born: 9 May 1907, Fulham, London
Died: 18 May 1953, Northampton

Batting

M	I	NO	Runs	Av
47	71	6	2338	35.96

50	100	ct/st		
12	5	20		

Bowling

Balls	Runs	Wkts	Av	5wI	10wM
30	31	0	-	-	-

Best Performances
206 v. Warwickshire at Lord's, 1931

The saturnine-looking Edgar Thomas Killick, a graceful and polished batter with a wide range of strokes, was once described as 'an England batsman if ever one wore a dog collar'. He was also a fine outfielder, quick to the ball and accurate in throw, but after a moderate Test bow against South Africa in 1929 he was ordained into the Church of England. Manifestly, he made the right decision, but one may think the Almighty owed England and Middlesex a lot of runs for the 1930s.

Killick enjoyed a fine career at Cambridge. He won his Blue in 1928, 1929 and 1930 and in the final year scored a match-winning hundred against Oxford. His most notable innings for Cambridge, however, was a marvellous unbeaten 200 against Glamorgan in 1929. This match-winning effort came in 200 minutes and included a century before lunch on the third day.

The highest of Killick's five Middlesex hundreds was 206 against Warwickshire at Lord's in 1931, a superb effort of some five and a half hours. Killick, who had recently been ordained and whose only appearance this was in the season, cut and pulled superbly and added 277 for the first wicket with Greville Stevens. Killick was involved in an even larger stand against Sussex at Hove, when he and Hendren added 301 for the third wicket, Killick's share being 140. Two weeks later, the pair added 195 for the same wicket against Surrey at The Oval, Killick scoring 170. Killick's last hundred came against Derbyshire at Lord's in 1932, a valuable 128 in 235 minutes, when he added 146 for the seventh wicket with George Hart after Tommy Mitchell had threatened to run through the innings. Another fine performance came against the 1929 South Africans at Lord's. Going in at 61-6 Killick was last out for 111, scored at one a minute, having helped take the score to 240.

For the last few years of his life, Killick was vicar at Bishop's Stortford and, sadly, he collapsed and died aged forty-six, while playing in an inter-diocesan match between Coventry and St Alban's at Northampton.

Amritt Harichand Latchman
RHB, LBG, 1965-1973

Born: 26 July 1943, Kingston, Jamaica

Batting

M	I	NO	Runs	Av
170	183	49	1950	14.55
12	9	3	88	14.66

50	100	ct/st
3	-	79
-	-	3

Bowling

Balls	Runs	Wkts	Av	5wI	10wM
22104	11032	400	27.58	18	1
444	342	9	38.00	-	-

Best Performances
96 v. Worcestershire at Kidderminster, 1972
45* v. Sussex at Bath, 1970
7-91 v. Pakistanis at Lord's, 1967
2-39 v. Lancashire at Lord's, 1971

Amritt Harichand Latchman (known as Harry) was that rare bird in modern county cricket, a genuine leg spinner with a googly. There were respected judges who felt that he should have trained on to Test level but Latchman never seemed to lose the tendency for spells of too erratic length and direction when the solving of this problem could have made the difference at top level. It was a big disappointment when he took his tossed up leg breaks to Trent Bridge and, too soon, out of the first-class game completely.

A local product, brought up and educated at Shepherd's Bush, Latchman began his county career on the highest note in 1965, achieving innings figures of 6 for 52 in 15.2 overs against Yorkshire at Lord's in his second match. What is more all Latchman's Yorkshire victims were, or were to become, Test players.

Latchman really established himself in 1967 when he took 67 wickets, average 26.14, and reached the pinnacle of his career against the Pakistan tourists in early July. According to *Wisden*, he spun and flighted like an experienced professional to attain first innings figures of 7 for 91 in 39 overs. An imaginative England selection panel would have immediately put him im the Test team, or at least taken him on the next overseas tour. They did neither and Latchman never really seemed to be in contention again, despite magnificent bowling the following season, when he had a career best return of 88 wickets, average 18.88, one of the few bright spots in a generally depressing season.

Sadly, the following two seasons were very much ones of anticlimax. Parfitt's captaincy seemed to have little place for unorthodox spin and a preference for non-stop seam. The assumption of the captaincy by Brearley in 1971 saw a renaissance as Latchman took 81 wickets but he then lost his way again and played no more for Middlesex after 1973. Here was a bowler with the ability to go far.

Henry William Lee

RHB, OB, 1933-1934

Born: 26 October 1890, Marylebone
Died: 21 April 1981, Westminster

Batting

M	I	NO	Runs	Av
401	666	45	18594	29.94
50	100	ct/st		
74	35	164		

Bowling

Balls	Runs	Wkts	Av	5wI	10wM
24487	11064	340	32.54	7	2

Best Performances

243* v. Nottinghamshire at Lord's, 1921
8-39 v. Gloucestershire at Cheltenham, 1923

Harry Lee was eldest of three brothers, locally born, who played for Middlesex. Frank and Jack moved to Somerset but Harry gave excellent service to his home county.

Lee's crouching stance and leg-side tendency did not make for the most attractive of batsmen, but he was for many years an ideal county opener and an admirable foil for faster scorers lower down.

Lee exceeded 1,000 runs 12 times between 1919 and 1932. Surprisingly, he never stretched to 2,000 but when compiling his season best 1,845 runs, average 36.90, in 1929 he not only scored more runs than anyone else but reputedly batted with more dash than previously.

Harry Lee's efforts were the more remarkable because he had one leg longer than the other as a result of a fractured thigh during the First World War.

Lee obtained 35 first-class centuries for Middlesex, and twice, against Surrey at The Oval in 1919 and against Sussex at Lord's in 1929, he scored one in each innings. His last, 119 against Warwickshire at Edgbaston in 1934, took 330 minutes and at 43 years and 299 days he was the county's second oldest century scorer at the time. One imagines it was compiled in much the same way as his first twenty years earlier.

Harry Lee went on to convert single centuries to 'doubles' four times. The highest was an epic 243* in over 6 hours against Nottinghamshire at Lord's in 1921. With G.E.V. Crutchley, Lee added 231 in 135 minutes for the first wicket as Middlesex went on to a Lord's record total for the county of 612-8 declared and an eventual innings win. In 1920, Lee compiled a match-deciding 6-hour unbeaten 221 against Hampshire at Southampton and in 1929 he registered two further 'doubles' including a 410-minute 225 against Surrey, he and 'Gubby' Allen adding 319 for the second wicket. Lee was also involved in four double-century opening stands (241 with Pelham Warner against Sussex in 1920 was the highest).

Lee played one Test match in an emergency in 1930/31 and was a first-class umpire and coach at Downside.

Robert Slade Lucas
RHB, RM, 1891-1900

Born: 17 July 1867, Teddington
Died: 5 January 1942, Haywards Heath, Sussex

Batting

M	I	NO	Runs	Av
73	120	7	2064	18.26

50	100	ct/st
6	1	33

Bowling

Balls	Runs	Wkts	Av	5wI	10wM
184	171	3	57.00	-	-

Best Performances
185 v. Sussex at Hove, 1895

Robert Slade Lucas was an orthodox amateur batsman who made a fair number of low scores but from time to time produced batting of undeniable class. His first innings of real value for Middlesex occurred against Surrey at The Oval in 1894. In their second innings, the county were a mere 2 runs on with 8 wickets down but Lucas was then joined by Jim Phillips and together they added 149 for the nineth wicket (a Middlesex record until 1919 and still the third-best stand for the ninth wicket) in 105 minutes before Lucas fell for 97. Three weeks later, Lucas played superbly for 135 minutes against Sussex at Hove, this time missing a first hundred by only one run, and scoring his runs out of 160, playing easily the best innings in a game won by 6 wickets.

The elusive century came in 1895, and again Sussex at Hove were the recipients. After a run of low scores, Lucas again showed his class with a brilliant 185 in 230 minutes, with 23 fours. Lucas and Tim O'Brien actually added 338 runs together. At the time it was a Middlesex record for any wicket, a record world-wide and it remains the county fifth-wicket record to this day, and the longest standing partnership record for Middlesex.

Lucas continued to appear with decreasing frequency and success until 1900. His general inconsistency amidst three brilliant innings appears to be inexplicable. Perhaps faults in concentration, or interests outside cricket were partly to blame; it is now impossible to say.

In 1894, Lucas toured America with Lord Hawke's side and the following year captained a privately organised tour to the West Indies, but from then on his form and frequency of appearances declined. Lucas was an excellent club batsman, and played for Old Merchant Taylors, as well as the Richmond and Teddington Clubs. He also played field hockey for Teddington.

Hon. Alfred Lyttelton

RHB, WKT, 1877-1887

Born: 7 February 1857, Westminster
Died: 5 July 1913, Marylebone

Batting

M	I	NO	Runs	Av
35	61	2	1656	28.06
50	**100**	**ct/st**		
6	3	46/19		

Bowling

Balls	Runs	Wkts	Av	5wI	10wM
112	74	0	-	-	-

Best Performances
181 v. Gloucestershire at Clifton, 1883

Alfred Lyttelton was a strong front-foot batsman described in contemporary sources as 'in the classical mould' and a gifted wicketkeeper chosen for England almost on merit. He also had one immortal bowling spell when he handed the wicketkeeping gloves to W.G. Grace in the 1884 Oval Test and took 4 wickets in 12 overs, bowling under-arm while still wearing his pads. They were his only first-class wickets.

Lyttelton first came to the forefront for Cambridge, winning his Blue 1876-79 and captaining in his last year. He also played for Gentlemen's and I Zingari teams as well as for Middlesex.

His Middlesex appearances were limited, but he performed sufficiently well to suggest that he was potentially one of the best batsmen wicketkeepers to play for the county. Lyttelton's day of glory came on 16 August 1883, the first day of the Gloucestershire match at Clifton. Lyttelton scored a career best 181 in about 4 hours, with 1 six and 21 fours. With his skipper Isaac Walker he added

324, the first stand of more than 300 for Middlesex, and in fact the best stand at that time in all first-class cricket. It was a Middlesex second-wicket record until 1914 and remains second on the list. Lyttelton hit two other hundreds for Middlesex, both against Nottinghamshire at Trent Bridge, in 1877 and 1879. In the latter instance he seems to have had early trouble piercing the field. Charles Thornton scored 72 out of 89 for the first wicket; when I.D. Walker was out 18 runs later for 18, opener Lyttelton had scored 15 out of 107.

Alfred, a son of the fourth Lord Lyttelton, was a superb all-round sportsman. He played soccer for England and won a Cup medal with Old Etonians. He also excelled at rackets, tennis and athletics. From 1895 to 1906 he was Conservative MP for Warwick then, until his death in 1913, he sat for St George's, Hanover Square. From 1903 to 1905, he was Colonial Secretary. His brother Edward appeared for Middlesex, and several other relations played various levels of first-class cricket.

Born: 13 August 1869, Merchiston, Edinburgh
Died: 20 August 1919, Marylebone

Batting

M	I	NO	Runs	Av
184	286	39	4846	19.61
50	**100**	**ct/st**		
17	2	280/111		

Bowling

Balls	Runs	Wkts	Av	5wI	10wM
-	-	-	-	-	-

Best Performances
141 v. Sussex at Lord's, 1897

Gregor MacGregor's wicketkeeping first drew wide acclaim while he was at Cambridge, when his lightening reflexes enabled him to take fast bowlers such as S.M.J. Woods while standing up to the wickets. His abilities were noted at top level and he played his first Test aged twenty, totalling 8 in all between 1890 and 1893. In 1891/92 he toured Australia under W.G. Grace; he did his best but seemed to find the fast true wickets unsuitable to his style and it is reported he added nothing to his reputation.

As he grew older and the reflexes deteriorated to something akin to normality (due in part to somewhat careless living) MacGregor lost some of his edge but he remained a valuable county wicketkeeper and from 1899 to 1907. He was a shrewd and mainly successful county captain, leading Middlesex to its first championship in 1903, and he was a confidant and friend to his talented professional bowlers such as Abert Trott and John Thomas Hearne.

MacGregor scored two centuries for Middlesex, both against Sussex. The first, at Lord's in 1897, was a fine 141, the best score by a Middlesex number 7 at that time. He also added 141 with Robert Lucas, the best seventh-wicket stand for the county until 1910.

MacGregor's other century was at Hove in 1905. Again batting at number 7 his 109, and a sixth-wicket stand of 130 with E.A. Beldam, saved their side from disaster, though they ultimately lost.

When Gregor MacGregor ceased playing in 1907 he was leading Middlesex wicketkeeper with regard to total dismissals. Even today he stands in 7th place, and his average number of dismissals per match – 2.13 – bears comparison with most. In all first-class cricket he scored 6,381 runs, av. 18.02, caught 411 and stumped 148 batsmen.

Apart from cricket, MacGregor was a fine rugby footballer, who won his Blue at Cambridge and from 1890 to 1894 played 13 times for Scotland.

Although he held the position of Middlesex honorary treasurer until his death and worked at the Stock Exchange, he rather lost his way in life in later years and his sad early death came as little surprise to many close to him.

Francis Thomas Mann

RHB, 1909-1931

Born: 3 March 1888, Winchmore Hill
Died: 6 October 1964, Milton-Lilbourne, Wiltshire

Batting

M	I	NO	Runs	Av
314	472	39	10656	24.60

50	100	ct/st		
53	8	137		

Bowling

Balls	Runs	Wkts	Av	5wl	10wM
178	172	2	43.00	-	-

Best Performances
194 v. Warwickshire at Edgbaston, 1926

Frank Mann, whose sons George and John both played for Middlesex, was a large and powerful man who hit the ball hard and often and captained the county from 1921 (when they were champions) until 1928.

An example of his hitting poweers came against Nottinghamshire at Lord's in 1921. Going in at number 8 against a tired attack, Mann reached 53 in 19 minutes from 20 balls and 13 scoring strokes. Only Jim Smith has bettered this for Middlesex. Mann could bat in a more orthodox fashion, as shown by his best-ever score, 194 against Warwickshire at Edgbaston in 1926, which took him more than 5 hours.

It is perhaps a little surprising that so regular a batsman as Frank Mann only reached 1,000 runs in a season on one occasion – 1923 – when he finished with 1,095 runs (av. 28.07) though he did come close in other seasons. In 1926 for instance, he scored 944 runs (av. 34.96) after seeming certain of reaching four figures until the last few weeks of the season.

Mann scored 8 centuries altogether for Middlesex, the first a blistering 135 in 165 minutes against Worcestershire in 1913, an innings which saved Middlesex from disaster but not, unfortunately, from defeat. The next best score was 35.

Another memorable piece of batting came when Middlesex scored 502-6 to beat Nottinghamshire at Trent Bridge in 1925, still a championship record for a winning fourth innings and Mann and Hendren added 271 unbeaten. This is still a Middlesex record for the seventh wicket and Mann's share was 101*. The same pair added 256 for the fourth wicket against Essex at Leyton in 1923, Mann hitting 122 of the runs, with 2 sixes and 14 fours.

Frank Mann won his Blue at Cambridge, and captained England in the five Tests in South Africa in 1922/23. In all first-class cricket he scored 13,235 runs, average 23.42.

Mann was Middlesex president from 1947 until 1949. He had an outstanding First World War in the Scots Guards and was three times mentioned in dispatches. In peacetime, he worked in the family brewing business.

Francis George Mann
RHB, 1937-1954

Born: 6 September 1917, Byfleet, Surrey
Died: 8 August 2001, London

Batting

M	I	NO	Runs	Av
54	147	9	3403	24.65
50	**100**	**ct/st**		
20	3	41		

Bowling

Balls	Runs	Wkts	Av	5wI	10wM
40	45	2	22.50	-	-

Best Performances
116 v. Nottinghamshire at Trent Bridge, 1948
2-16 v. Sussex at Hove, 1939

Old Etonian George Mann, son of Frank, won his Cambridge Blue as an aggressive middle-order batsman (with a marked leg-side bias) and inspirational fielder, before more pressing matters interrupted what seemed like a burgeoning career of some promise. He more than did his bit in the war, returning home with a DSO and MC.

Mann's subsequent career never really took off as had been hoped. His batting never developed as many thought it should have done, especially after the coaching he had been given at school while his cricket career was finally truncated through business calls in the family brewery.

Mann still left his mark on Middlesex and England cricket, however, despite a mere 84 appearances for his county, for which he was capped in 1939 and which he led in 1948 and 1949 to third and joint-first positions. Mann scored 3 centuries for his county, and all were fine innings which affected the game markedly. In 1947 he scored 106, and he and Denis Compton added 304 in 3 hours and 15 minutes, a stand which remains the second best for the fourth wicket for the county.

Mann and Compton's dashing strokeplay put Middlesex into an overwhelmingly strong position. In 1948 Compton and Mann were involved in another good stand, 122 for the fourth wicket in 80 minutes against Leicestershire at Lord's but the most newsworthy batting concerned the last wicket. Mann was on 77 when joined by Laurie Gray. The last wicket added 43, with Mann finally being out for 114; Gray was then still unbeaten on 0. A few weeks later Mann scored 116 against Notts at Trent Bridge. He and Edrich added 163 in 135 minutes to set up Middlesex for an innings win.

George Mann played for and captained England in seven Tests. His record of 376 runs, av. 37.60, with a fine 136* at Port Elizabeth in 1948/49 as its peak suggests a better batsman than his county record may tend to indicate.

George Mann became a busy administrator, successively honorary treasurer, chairman and, from 1983 to 1990, president of Middlesex. In 1984/85 he was president of MCC, and his service on the Cricket Council and the TCCB led to his being appointed CBE.

Alan Edward Moss
RHB, RF, 1950-1963

Born: 14 November 1930, Tottenham

Batting

M	I	NO	Runs	Av
307	329	141	1234	6.56
50	100	ct/st		
-	-	121		

Bowling

Balls	Runs	Wkts	Av	5wI	10wM
51135	21556	1088	19.81	59	12

Best Performances
40 v. Surrey at The Oval, 1952
8-31 v. Northamptonshire at Kettering, 1960

Alan Moss was a tall and strong pace bowler who first suggested something out of the ordinary with regard to cricketing potential while doing his National Service in the RAF. On his return to county cricket, he built up his speed so that at his peak he was genuinely quick and on a helpful wicket could generate considerable pace off the wicket.

Moss played 307 games for Middlesex, more than any other player for the county who relied solely on pace bowling throughout his career. He was capped in 1952 and given a benefit in 1962. The following season, with his fitness uncertain, he resigned and went into business.

The feeling that Moss may have been Middlesex's best-ever pace bowler is confirmed by the fact that he took many more wickets for the county than any other pure paceman (Jack Durston turned to spin in later years), and took five wickets in an innings and 10 in a match more than any other fast bowler too.

Moss four times exceeded 100 wickets for the county and he reached his peak with a magnificent return of 118 wickets, average 12.84, in 1960. Middlesex finished in third place that season and Moss had much to do with the county's best placing since their 1949 championship season. Three times in 1960 Moss took 7 or more wickets in an innings. The best, and it remained his career best, was a magnificent 8 for 31 in 21 overs against Northamptonshire at Kettering. So brilliantly did Moss bowl on a previously none too helpful pitch that Northamptonshire saw a first innings deficit of only 72 subside to an innings defeat. Moss's match figures were 11 for 91, impressive enough, but a few weeks earlier, against Glamorgan at Neath Moss turned on another match-winning performance, when he added 8 for 37 to his first innings figures of 5 for 14. His match figures of 13 for 51 were, and remained, his best ever. In fact taking the wickets:runs ratio they were arguably the best match figures for any Middlesex bowler.

Even late in his career, Moss remained formidable in the right conditions despite some loss of pace. In 1962, a generally indifferent season for both player and county, Moss had first innings figures of 8 for 55 against Gloucestershire and in 1963, with retirement in the offing, Gloucestershire were again the victims at Lord's in late August. A damp pitch on the first day saw Gloucestershire collapse as Moss took 8 for 40; his match figures of 10 for 60 were paramount in the Middlesex win, their last with Moss playing for them. Gloucestershire at Lord's tended in fact to be Moss's rabbits since he achieved his only hattrick against them, in 1956, when the distinguished trio of Young, Crapp and Emmett were his victims.

Alan Moss' career record in all matches was 1,301 wickets, average 20.78; his record for 9 Tests was 21 wickets, 29.80. It was surely desperately unfortunate for him that in his best years England's quick-bowling resources were probably at an all-time peak and he was never regarded as a frontline Test-match bowler. A decade before or after may have shown a different story. Perhaps better results with the bat may also have helped his prospects. As things were, infinitesimal ability and even less apparent ambition produced a run total which was so little more than his wickets to suggest that over a long career this was one of the poorest batsmen ever to appear for the Metropolitan county.

A.C. Walton (left) and A.E. Moss walk out to bat.

John Thomas Murray

RHB, WKT, 1952-1975

Born: 1 April 1935, Kensington, London

Batting

M	I	NO	Runs	Av
508	761	105	15251	23.24
132	119	18	2064	20.43

50	100	ct/st		
64	11	1024/199		
8	-	145/32		

Bowling

Balls	Runs	Wkts	Av	5wI	10wM
203	134	4	33.50	-	-
-	-	-	-	-	-

Best Performances

133* v. Oxford University at Oxford, 1963
75* v. Derbyshire at Chesterfield, 1973

John Murray first impressed as the seventeen-year-old deputy to the injured Leslie Compton in 1952. In 1956, he was regarded with sufficient respect to be awarded a cap and 10 years later he had a benefit; eventually he was appointed CBE for his cricket service. This neatly sums up the career of one of the most thorough-going professionals ever to grace the Middlesex team, from his neat turn out, which saw him straighten his cap and check his gloves seemingly after every ball, to the quiet technical excellence of his 'keeping. Only an occasional tendency to land awkwardly when diving far to his left or right when taking wide snicks, risking shoulder problems, suggested itself as any sort of weakness. Murray was a credit to his trade and a role model for any young cricketer wishing to become a full-time practitioner of the wicket-keeper's profession. What is more, Murray usually moved with a quiet economy which belied the difficulties of the job.

Unsurprisingly, John Murray is high on the lists with regard to Middlesex wicketkeeping feats. He holds the record – which is frankly likely to stand for all time – for the number of dismissals in a season, 99 in 1960. In 1957, he had moved into second place to Fred Price with 87, but he covered himself with more glory that season when in all matches he achieved a century of dismissals and also scored more than 1,000 runs.

Murray exceeded 70 dismissals in a season 7 times, more than any other 'keeper for the county. As for Murray's career total of 1,223 dismissals (1,024 catches, 199 stumpings) this places him top of the Middlesex list by far; Fred Price, another stalwart, is second with 938.

In 1965, Murray achieved 9 dismissals in the match against Hampshire at Lord's, equalling Montague Turner 90 years earlier. They remain joint record holders, as do Murray and Fred Price for the number of stumpings in a match. Murray had 5 against Sussex at Hove in 1973.

So accomplished was Murray's 'keeping that there is perhaps a tendency to ignore the fact that he was a good enough batsman to score more than 15,000 runs and 11 centuries for the county. He exceeded 1,000 runs four times, with 1,127 (av. 31.30) in 1964 his best return. Invariably playing straight with unfussy orthodoxy, he played some fine innings, none more so than his century against Yorkshire at Headingley in 1964. He and Bennett added 220 unbroken for the seventh wicket. Otherwise, sadly, Middlesex were completely, almost embarrassingly, outplayed. Murray and Bennett also added 182 for this wicket against Glamorgan at Lord's in 1961, another stand which saved their side from near disaster.

In first-class cricket as a whole, Murray overtook H. Strudwick in 1975 to become the most prolific wicketkeeper of all time. His final total of 1,527 was subsequently overtaken by Herbert Strudwick and Bob Taylor but he deserves his solid second placing. As a Test player Murray played 21 times, scoring 506 runs with 1 century and obtaining 55 dismissals. Somehow he rarely seemed at home in the worldwide game that is Test cricket. His métier was that of a Middlesex and Lord's professional. Possibly the training he received at headquarters did not quite equip him for the wider cricket world; perhaps he was unwittingly stifled. He seemed to be a slightly discontented tourist and certainly he appeared far from happy in his short spell as an England Test selector.

John Murray hits a ball to leg from Jim Laker in the Middlesex v. International Cavaliers match at Lord's.

Harry Robert Murrell

RHB, WKT, 1906-1926

Born: 19 November 1879, Hounslow
Died: 15 August 1952, West Wickham, Kent

Batting

M	I	NO	Runs	Av
342	467	58	6033	14.75
50	**100**	**ct/st**		
20	-	517/261		

Bowling

Balls	Runs	Wkts	Av	5wl	10wM
48	44	0	-	-	-

Best Performances
96* v. Essex at Leyton, 1919

Although from Hounslow, Joe Murrell (real name Harry Robert) had to go to Kent before being taken on by his native county, for whom he became the first of a line of fine professional wicketkeepers.

Murrell, tall and spare of build, was a good all-round 'keeper but especially adept at leg side takes. This was partly due to his having a strong left-side bias but does not explain a similar proficiency with left-handed batsmen; perhaps unusually quick reflexes enter the equation here. Though rarely above the 'tail', Murrell was also an aggressive batsman with a range of vigorous off-side strokes. Possibly he was really a natural left-hander.

Against Hampshire at Southampton in 1921, Murrell hit 50 in 15 minutes but his highest score was 96 not out made when he and E. Martin added 152 for the nineth wicket against Essex at Leyton in 1919 in 75 minutes, then a Middlesex nineth-wicket record, and still second on the list. Another memorable stand had been made against Nottinghamshire at Lord's in 1913 when Murrell, who finished 71*, joined M.H.C.

Doll to add 182 unbeaten. It remains the county eighth-wicket record. Given such performances it is a surprise, and a pity, he never reached a century.

Joe Murrell's wicketkeeping was known more for solid consistency than brilliance, but was probably none the worse for that. Against Gloucestershire at Bristol in 1926, he became the first Middlesex wicketkeeper to have 6 victims in an innings, a total only beaten once. His 78 victims in 1911, remained a record for 26 years. His 24 stumpings that season were not beaten until 1929. To this day he is 4th on the list. Murrell's 778 dismissals is third best for his county, well ahead of any rivals.

After retirement Murrell remained at Lord's, and for many years he was Middlesex scorer. A serious-minded individual who thought a lot about matters outside cricket, Murrell was reputed to be an ardent socialist. This was at a time when not to be so showed selfishness, ignorance or lack of humanity. One doubts Murrell could have been faulted on any of these.

Born: 5 November 1861, Dublin
Died: 9 December 1948, Ramsey, Isle of Man

Batting

M	I	NO	Runs	Av
156	268	19	7377	29.62

50	100	ct/st
43	10	111/2

Bowling

Balls	Runs	Wkts	Av	5wI	10wM
529	272	2	136.00	-	-

Best Performances
202 v. Sussex at Hove, 1895

One of the few *bona fide* Irishmen to play county cricket, Sir Timothy O'Brien was strongly built and confident, an outstanding forcing batsman with some fast-scoring epics to his credit. Outstanding among these was his brilliant 100 not out in 80 minutes, with 14 fours, his last 83 runs coming in 35 minutes which paved the way for a dazzling and unexpected win over Yorkshire at Lord's in 1889. He had gone in at 129-4, with 150 still needed, but the runs were scored in quick time with only 2 more wickets lost. O'Brien had scored 92 in the first innings so enjoyed a triumphant match.

O'Brien's highest score and only double century was 202 against Sussex at Hove in 1895. He was at the wickets only 4 hours and hit 27 fours. O'Brien added 338 in 195 minutes in a stand with Slade Lucas – a Middlesex fifth-wicket record to this day, at the time a record Middlesex stand for any wicket, and also at the time a fifth-wicket record world-wide. Two years earlier, Middlesex had been forced to follow on by Surrey at Lord's but a marvellous second innings opening stand of 228 in 150 minutes (a Middlesex

record at the time) by O'Brien, who was skippering the team, and Andrew Ernest Stoddart paved the way for an unexpected victory. O'Brien's team turned a 179 first innings deficit into a 79-run win; little wonder a large crowd assembled outside the pavilion to cheer the players.

O'Brien, who gained his Blue at Oxford in 1884 and 1885, played 5 Test matches for England between 1884 and 1895/96. He enjoyed little batting success but did lead a winning side on his only appearance as captain.

After giving up with Middlesex O'Brien played for a number of years for the Ireland team, then still known as 'Gentlemen', and he led them on one occasion. He was still not finished. In his last first-class match for Lionel Robinson's team against Oxford in 1914 he scored 90 and 111 'in fine style' according to *Wisden*. He was then fifty-two years old, but this father of ten children remained potent and vigorous right until the day he died.

Born: 8 December 1936, Billingford, Norfolk

Batting

M	I	NO	Runs	Av
387	665	84	21304	36.66
75	72	3	1506	21.82

50	100	ct/st		
114	46	452		
5	2	17		

Bowling

Balls	Runs	Wkts	Av	5wI	10wM
14405	6424	231	27.80	4	-
946	689	34	20.26	-	-

Best Performances

200* v. Nottinghamshire at Trent Bridge, 1964
119 v. Nottinghamshire at Trent Bridge, 1969
6-45 v. Oxford University at Oxford, 1969
4-2 v. Gloucestershire at Lydney, 1970

Peter Parfitt showed great early promise as an aggressive left-hander, a brilliant fielder, and possibilities as an off spinner. In the event, his batting made the grade though sometimes he was strangely indecisive and seemingly unwilling to play his shots.

Parfitt's 46 centuries in 665 innings for the county shows he was a regular hundreds man and especially earlier in his career they were usually most attractively made. His only double century, 200*, was made against Nottinghamshire at Trent Bridge in 1964, and his 21 fours in five and a half hours was a match-winning effort. Parfitt seemed to enjoy Trent Bridge, since he scored 105 and 101 not out in the match against Nottinghamshire there in 1961. The following season he scored 122 and 114 against the Pakistani tourists at Lord's (and in his next innings hit 101* for England against the same side at Trent Bridge).

Parfitt exceeded 1,000 runs for Middlesex in 14 seasons successively, an unbroken run beaten only by 'Patsy' Hendren. It is an impressive record yet his form was sometimes surprisingly uneven, his game seemingly lacking in conviction. His best season was 1961, when he scored 2,007 runs, average 39.35. At that time, Parfitt batted with a freedom and panache he was never to consistently match in subsequent years.

Parfitt was arguably the most reliable close catcher ever to play for the county. He finished third overall and only John Donald Carr, with many fewer games, exceeds his career average of 1.17 victims per match. With 46 catches in 1960 and 1966, 45 in 1968 and 43 in 1967 he holds the top four places for the county for seasons' totals. The off spin was useful but underused in his formative years.

As captain from 1968 to 1970, Parfitt was none too convincing and the team's fortunes declined under him. His Test record for 37 matches – 1,882 runs, average 40.91 – looks good but he often failed against the stronger attacks. A bubbly, sociable character, Parfitt has lately organised hospitality at major sporting occasions.

Ian Alexander Ross Peebles
RHB, LBG/OB, 1928-1948

Born: 20 January 1908, Aberdeen
Died: 27 February 1980, Speen, Bucks.

Batting

M	I	NO	Runs	Av
165	222	70	1361	8.95

50	100	ct/st
I	-	120

Bowling

Balls	Runs	Wkts	Av	5wI	10wM
27991	12122	610	19.87	40	8

Best Performances
58 v. Oxford University at Oxford, 1938
8-24 v. Worcestershire at Worcester, 1930

Ian Peebles was first spotted as a thirteen year old with a natural talent for 'googly' bowling, and he later worked at the Faulkner cricket school, with ample opportunity to learn all aspects of bowling. He was sent on the MCC tour of South Africa in 1927/28 without any county experience; supposedly secretary to the captain R.T. Stanyforth, he played regularly. For a while one of the most effective slow bowlers in English cricket he soon lost the ability to bowl anything but the 'googly', the surprise element had gone and by the age of twenty-three, Peebles was already firmly on the way downhill. Many spinners reach an early peak – Peebles was an extreme example.

At his peak, Ian Peebles was a fine bowler. A tall man, he had a high and flowing action. He used subtle variations and until he lost his leg break he mixed this with a well-disguised and well-spun googly.

Peebles' finest performances came early and his best bowling was against Worcestershire at Worcester in 1930, when he was twenty-two.

He followed his first innings 5 for 48 with a match-winning 8 for 24 in 19.1 overs and with his last 19 deliveries he took 4 wickets for 4 runs. Both his innings figures and match figures (13-72) remained his best. Another outstanding performance came against Gloucestershire at Lord's in 1932 when he took 5 wickets for 2 runs with his last 11 balls, a hat-trick included.

Peebles took 117 wickets (av. 19.47) in 1929, his first full season, and he repeated the century in 1931, after which such form proved completely beyond him. In 13 Tests, his last aged twenty-three, Peebles took 45 wickets, average 30.91.

Peebles was normally of little account with the bat but against Kent at Canterbury in August 1939 he was junior partner in a pretty sensational last-wicket stand of 116. Jim Smith made 98 of them, Peebles' share was 14.

Peebles led the side in 1939, but a lost eye during the war finished his career, though he became a good and entertaining cricket writer, and also went into the wine trade.

James Phillips

RHB, RM, 1890-1898

Born: 1 September 1860 (or 1851), Pleasant Creek, Victoria
Died: 21 April 1930, Vancouver, Canada

Batting

M	I	NO	Runs	Av
90	144	42	1152	11.29
50	100	ct/st		
2	-	33		

Bowling

Balls	Runs	Wkts	Av	5wI	10wM
10172	4924	221	22.28	16	4

Best Performances
67* v. Surrey at The Oval, 1894
8-69 v. Kent at Lord's, 1895

Jim Phillips has an interesting place in cricket history as the first umpire famed for being just that, but he was also an excellent cricketer who played for Victoria in Australia and Canterbury in New Zealand as well as enjoying several successful seasons with Middlesex.

'Dimboola Jim' was an Australian backwoodsman who did not play serious cricket until well into his twenties – at least. An 1860 birth year now seems to be accepted but at one time 1851 was suggested, meaning he would have been approaching his fortieth year when first playing for Middlesex.

Whatever his age, Phillips became a sound and watchful batsman and a medium-pace bowler relying on accuracy of pitch and flight rather than spiteful spin. His best analysis for the county was 8 for 69 against Kent at Lord's in 1895. He took 10 wickets altogether and he and J.T. Hearne in tandem ensured an innings win. Phillips was having a pretty good run since in the previous game only days earlier, against Lancashire at Lord's, his figures of 7 for 56 were in no way to blame for an innings

defeat. 1895 was Phillips' best season, with 48 wickets, average 17.12, but perhaps his most decisive bowling came against Sussex at Lord's in 1892, when his match figures of 13-117 decimated the opposition. He also took 13 wickets against Gloucestershire at Lord's 1896, another match-deciding performance.

As a batsman for Middlesex his average is moderate, but he did help Slade Lucas add 149 for the ninth wicket against Surrey in 1894 (at the time a record) and actually scored 110* in a first-class match for Canterbury against Wellington in 1898/99 aged thirty-eight, or forty-seven, or whatever.

In the 1880s and 1890s Phillips made a name as the best umpire in cricket up to that time, and he played a big, in fact almost a lone part in the rooting out of 'bowlers' with suspect actions. His bravery in 'calling' Australia's Ernest Jones at Melbourne in 1897/98 was a huge landmark for cricket, and umpires everywhere.

A mining engineer, Phillips emigrated to Canada and reputedly died a wealthy man.

John Sidney Ernest Price
LHB, RF, 1961-1975

Born: 22 July 1937, Harrow

Batting

M	I	NO	Runs	Av
242	190	80	902	8.20
124	67	38	240	8.27

50	100	ct/st
-	-	89
-	-	23

Bowling

Balls	Runs	Wkts	Av	5wl	10wM
36773	16440	734	22.39	25	4
6276	3582	192	18.65	1	-

Best Performances
41* v. Cambridge University at Fenner's, 1969
14 v. Surrey at The Oval, 1971
8-48 v. Derbyshire at Lord's, 1966
6-34 v. Surrey at The Oval, 1971

John 'Sport' Price caused something of a stir in 1961, his debut season, when he came, as an amateur, straight from Wembley CC. Strongly built with a good body action, Price tended to skid through rather than gain lift from the pitch but in his early years at least he possessed that rare commodity, genuine, albeit sometimes somewhat raw, pace. For much of his career Price also had a most unusual crescent-shaped run up which would tend to put a deal of stress on one side of his body and doubtless caused some of the minor injuries to which Price was prone.

It was largely due to the reduction in the number of matches played that Price never took 100 wickets in a season, but his highest tally, 94, average 18.74, in 1966 represented a very good effort indeed. In a poor season for the county, and despite fitness problems, he bowled with fire and aggression, often proving to be the side's only effective bowler. It was during 1966 that Price produced his best innings figures, when bowling with fire and straightness he skittled Derbyshire at Lord's

and his analysis of 8 for 48 in 26 overs included 6 batsmen being clean bowled. In 1970, Price had another 'golden' match when taking full advantage of a Lord's pitch giving lift. His lightening deliveries accounted for 8 Kent batsmen for 56 in the first innings and a further 6 for 33 second time around, for match figures of 14 for 89 as the hop county slumped to a heavy defeat. Kent's David Nicholls had a particularly unhappy match, bagging a 'King Pair', each time falling to Price without the intervention of a fielder.

Price seemed to show little interest or ambition with the bat, and one or two of his season's averages were ridiculously low. However, his out fielding, marked by speedy pick-up and flat and accurate return, made him a big asset to his county, and specially valuable in limited-overs cricket.

Price played 15 Tests over eight and a half years. 40 wickets at 35.02 may not seem impressive, but one doubts that he had a proper chance.

Wilfred Frederick Frank Price
RHB, WKT, 1926-1947

Born: 25 April 1902, Westminster
Died: 13 January 1969, Hendon

Batting

M	I	NO	Runs	Av
382	555	96	8300	18.08

50	100	ct/st
33	3	627/311

Bowling

Balls	Runs	Wkts	Av	5wI	10wM
-	-	-	-	-	-

Best Performances
111 v. Worcestershire at Dudley, 1933

Fred Price was a more than competent all-round wicketkeeper, but specially adept at leg-side takes, when quick reflexes as well as technical proficiency are required.

Fred Price succeeded Joe Murrell as the regular wicketkeeper and when the position was causing difficulty in 1947 he came back aged forty-five and did himself infinite credit. He was capped in 1928 and when he finally laid down the gloves (so to speak) his total of 938 dismissals was a Middlesex record. In 2002 he is still second only to John Murray and likely to stay in that position for all time. A record Price does hold is total number of stumpings in a career, and here again the likelihood of anyone beating his tally of 311 is somewhat remote.

Apart from his patent consistency Fred Price was capable of some particularly brilliant performances, none more so than the 7 dismissals, all catches (a county record), which he made in the first innings of the Yorkshire game at Lord's in 1937. Price followed this rare feat by sharing in a century opening stand with R.E.C. Butterworth as the mighty Tykes slumped to a rare innings defeat. Price achieved six catches in an innings against Warwickshire the following season. Another great perfomance came against the South Africans in 1935 when his 8 match dismissals included 5 stumpings, still not bettered by a Middlesex wicketkeeper.

Fred Price had 91 dismissals in 1937, a county record until beaten by Murray in 1960. His 36 stumpings in 1929 remain inviolate; Price himself is second on the list with 26 in both 1934 and 1937.

Price was also a good enough batsman to open and score 3 centuries. His best score and maiden hundred, 111 against Worcestershire at Dudley in 1933, was also memorable for him and Patsy Hendren adding 332 runs together. It was the fourth-highest stand for Middlesex for any wicket at that time, yet not a fifth-wicket record. Then there was the 107 added for the last wicket against Sussex at Lord's in 1930 with H.J. Enthoven. Price's share was 3*.

A first-class umpire for 18 years, officiating in 8 Tests, he 'called' Tony Lock in 1952, an example which if followed might have saved trouble, and heartache in subsequent years.

Clive Thornton Radley

RHB, 1964-1987

Born: 13 May 1944, Hertford

Batting

M	I	NO	Runs	Av
520	813	132	24147	35.45
393	378	46	10081	30.36

50	100	ct/st
124	42	193
55	6	136

Bowling

Balls	Runs	Wkts	Av	5wI	10wM
270	156	8	19.50	-	-
25	20	1	-	-	-

Best Performances
200 v. Northamptonshire at Uxbridge, 1985
133* v. Glamorgan at Lord's, 1969
2-38 v. Glamorgan at Cardiff, 1985

Clive Radley, a fair-haired, grafting fighter of a batsman proved that guts and a natural ability to time the ball to perfection to just beat the field could get a county batsman to the top of his trade.

Clive Radley made 520 appearances for Middlesex, third only to Titmus and Hendren and he played a large part in the county's resurgence of the 1970s. A dab here, a smear there did not always make for scintillating viewing yet the score was always kept ticking over – an ability which made him a particularly successful limited-overs batsman – and his final career total placed him 6th heaviest Middlesex scorer all-time. Radley scored 42 centuries, the vast majority of them below 120, and he had to wait until his twenty-first season before registering his first and only 'double'. Appropriately, perhaps, it was exactly 200. A suitably low-key affair lasting 382 minutes, played in the 'wilds' of Uxbridge, it was also a match-winning knock which included a stand of 289 with Paul Downton, the third best for the fifth wicket.

Radley was involved in his share of big stands; the first was one of 227 for the sixth wicket with Fred Titmus against the 1965 South Africans. At the time, it was the county's best for this wicket and their best for any wicket against a touring team. It remains second on both counts. The feat almost passed without notice as Radley scored his maiden century. When it was beaten in 1983 against the New Zealanders, Gatting's partner in a third-wicket stand of 318 was Clive Radley (of course).

Radley exceeded 1,000 runs for the county 14 times, yet his best tally was 'only' 1,491, average 57.34, in 1980. There seemed something almost apologetic in the way Radley scored his runs yet to average 48.10 in an 8-match Test career suggests there was nothing for which to apologise.

Finally, almost without anyone noticing, Radley held 486 catches for the county – fewer than Patsy Hendren but more than anyone else in Middlesex history.

Mark Ravin Ramprakash
RHB, RM, 1987-2000

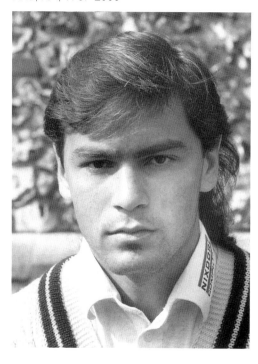

Born: 5 September 1969, Bushey, Herts.

Batting

M	I	NO	Runs	Av
211	345	47	15046	50.48
254	244	37	7825	37.80

50	100	ct/st
73	46	112
50	7	90

Bowling

Balls	Runs	Wkts	Av	5wl	10wM
1876	1101	19	57.94	-	-
1315	966	36	26.83	1	-

Best Performances
235 v. Yorkshire at Headingley, 1995
147* v. Worcestershire at Lord's, 1990
3-32 v. Glamorgan at Lord's, 1998
5-38 v. Leicestershire at Lord's, 1993

On style and technique one of the most impressive of Middlesex batsmen, his county record confirmed that for once looks were translated into runs. Ramprakash emphasised his potential right from his first-class debut, as a seventeen-year-old schoolboy, against Yorkshire at Lord's in 1987 when his second innings unbeaten 63 from 99 balls, and a stand of 116 with Roseberry, prevented disaster, though not, ultimately, defeat. Perhaps this match epitomised his career; good, stylish but rarely match-winning runs, but when Ramprakash threw in his lot with Surrey after 2000 he was only the second Middlesex batsman with a career average above 50. Only Denis Compton (7.24) beats his figure of a century every 7.5 innings; 7th equal with Warner and Parfitt with 46 centuries, they played far more matches.

Ramprakash exceeded 1,000 runs 8 times. In 1995 he scored 2,157 runs, average 89.87 with 10 centuries, reaching 2,000 ten days after his twenty-sixth birthday and finishing with 1,630 runs in 15 championship innings. There had been no scoring like it since the heyday of Compton and Edrich. He scored 5 double centuries, the first, 233 against Surrey at Lord's in 1992 aged twenty-two and a half; only Denis Compton, in 1939, has scored a double ton younger. His best score was 235 from 426 balls against Yorkshire at Headingley in 1995. This followed 214 from 337 balls against Surrey, and 205 from 295 balls, against Sussex, both at Lord's, earlier in the season.

Twice he scored 3 successive centuries, in 1990 and 1995, both spells including two hundreds in a match. Opening against Kent at Lord's in 1997 he carried his bat for 113 out of 256. Ramprakash scored centuries against all 17 other counties, emulating Gatting among Middlesex players.

Despite his heavy scoring, his career was somehow tinged with disappointment. He was a singularly unsuccessful county captain from 1997 to 1999, while he never established himself for England despite every opportunity.

John Thomas Rawlin
RHB, RMF, 1889-1909

Born: 10 November 1856, Greasborough,
Rotherham, Yorkshire
Died: 19 January 1924, Greasborough

Batting

M	I	NO	Runs	Av
229	358	31	5680	17.37
50	**100**	**ct/st**		
25	1	159		

Bowling

Balls	Runs	Wkts	Av	5wI	10wM
36571	13277	659	20.14	35	11

Best Performances
100 v. Surrey at Lord's, 1899
8-29 v. Gloucestershire at Clifton, 1893

John ('Turkey') Rawlin played a handful of games for his native Yorkshire before coming to Middlesex. He was thirty-two when he made his debut and fifty-two when making his last appearance in 1909. He remains the county's oldest County championship player.

Rawlin was a very sound batsman, of the type adept at keeping an end up during a crisis rather than winning matches with an exhibition of stroke play. Perhaps his only century was a contradiction. Aged forty-two, he scored exactly 100 in 150 minutes against Surrey at Lord's in 1899, laying the foundations for a good first-innings lead and eventual victory.

'Turkey's' medium-fast bowling, delivered with a high action moved slightly either way and came off the pitch with sufficient life to regularly rind the knuckles. In the days of a restricted fixture list, Rawlin never took 100 wickets. His best in a season was 90, average 14.36, in 1894. His best innings analysis was 8 for 29 v. Gloucestershire at Clifton in 1893, when one of his victims was W.G. Grace.

Rawlin's match figures of 12 for 79 did a great deal to win the match. Rawlin also had a match-winning 8 for 64 against Somerset at Taunton in 1891, after 7 for 35 in the Lord's match. He took the 'Cider County' for 18 for 150 in this season, yet perhaps more satisfying was 8 for 52 (innings) and 12 for 65 (match) to beat his native county at Headingley in 1892. Rawlin also took Yorkshire in 1894 – 8 for 50 in the first innings, 12 for 85 in the match, though here his joy would hardly have been boundless since Middlesex lost the match.

This remarkably loyal Lord's servant was on the staff there for more than twenty years. He played a number of games for MCC and in 1902, aged forty-five, scored 122 not out for them against London county. Even after retirement, when he returned to Yorkshire to resume his trade as a carpenter, he called his house in Greasborough 'Middlesex House'.

James Robertson

RHB, RF, 1878-1891

Born: 10 November 1850, Wardieburn,
    Edinburgh
Died: 21 March 1927, Kensington, London

Batting

M	I	NO	Runs	Av
102	164	32	1333	10.09
50	100	ct/st		
2	-	74		

Bowling

Balls	Runs	Wkts	Av	5wl	10wM
15998	6367	289	22.03	13	1

Best Performances
62 v. Surrey at Lord's, 1888
8-48 v. Nottinghamshire at Lord's, 1887

A tall and athletically-built Scot who played cricket for Edinburgh Academy but failed in his quest for a Blue at Oxford, Robertson became well known with Middlesex for his quick round-arm bowling, as well as his useful aggressive batting and good slip fielding.

Robertson was aged twenty-seven before his Middlesex debut in 1878 but he immediately made up for lost time with innings figures of 6 for 22 in 112 balls in his first bowl, against Surrey at Lord's. Later the same season, match figures of 10 for 84 against Yorkshire at Sheffield sent the Tykes plunging to an ignominious innings defeat. In the next match against the Australian tourists, he dismissed Bailey, Boyle and Allan in 4 balls to conclude the Australian second innings.

The following season's figures of 5 for 31 against Gloucestershire at Lord's included the wickets of both W.G. Grace and Fred Grace. Then in 1881, in an otherwise indifferent season, he had career best figures of 8 for 48 against Nottinghamshire at Lord's.

More fine bowling continued down the years, with Robertson not averse to long and statistically indifferent spells in unsympathetic conditions. He often did well against Surrey and 5 for 20 at Lord's in 1885 was an especially good effort in a losing cause. In 1886 Robertson bowled superbly against Nottinghamshire at Trent Bridge, achieving first innings figures of 7 for 35, without requiring any help from his fielders. In 1887, Robertson was even more effective. Second innings figures of 6 for 41 against Gloucestershire again included W.G. Grace as a victim and he had a career-best season's tally of 42 wickets.

James Robertson's career bowling record suggests that he was a very fine performer whose chance came later than it should. His batting too was not without its occasional value. His highest score of 62, against Surrey at Lord's in 1888, came out of an innings total of 159. In a dire Middlesex batting performance leading to an innings defeat, Robertson scored more in one innings than any of his colleagues scored in their two attempts.

John David Benbow Robertson
RHB, OB, 1937-1959

Born: 22 February 1907, Chiswick
Died: 12 October 1996, Bury St Edmunds, Suffolk

Batting

M	I	NO	Runs	Av
423	745	39	27088	38.36

50	100	ct/st		
129	59	301		

Bowling

Balls	Runs	Wkts	Av	5wl	10wM
4649	2006	56	35.82	-	-

Best Performances
331* v. Worcestershire at Lord's, 1949
4-37 v. Leicestershire at Leicester, 1955

John David Benbow Robertson watched Middlesex with his father at a very early age and as he progressed through his youthful training it seemed inevitable that here was a future Middlesex batsman. He let no-one down. Despite a quiet and modest demeanour, almost to the point of self-effacement (in retirement he omitted himself from a list of Middlesex openers, but included inarguably lesser batsmen, and the omission was genuine) he scored more runs and centuries than any other Middlesex opening batsman and obtained the highest individual score.

Jack Robertson's batting was all style. It was impossible for him ever to have made a graceless batting movement, nor did he seem to do anything but 'stroke' the ball. Such was his timing he had little need of the 'forcing' shot, still less the wild 'hoick'. Nonetheless, he often scored quickly; his record unbeaten 331 at Worcester in 1949 was obtained in a day. Legend has it that on leaving the ground he found he had a puncture. 'Its my unlucky day' was his exclamation. Robertson also had a sense of humour.

Jack Robertson's unbeaten 331 came in the 390 minutes of the first day's play. He hit 2 sixes and 39 fours and was involved in 4 century stands. He scored 3 other double

centuries, including 229 against Hampshire in 1947. Lasting just over 5 hours, it was more than the total of either Hampshire innings and a genuine match-winner. Robertson scored 59 centuries in all, to put him 6th on the county list, while his 27,088 runs (av. 38.36) give him 4th place. In every season between 1939 and 1958, Robertson exceeded 1,500 runs for the county and four times he went on to 2,000. He reached his peak in 1951 with 2,622 runs, average 62.43, when he passed fifty 25 times, a Middlesex record. His total runs even beat his stirling 1947 efforts – 2,328 runs (55.43). Robertson actually reached 2,000 runs in all first-class cricket every season 1946-52, a record of consistency unique and almost beyond belief.

It is possibly a little surprising that Robertson only once scored a century in each innings – 147 and 137 v. Sussex at Lord's in 1948 – but twice, in 1947 and 1954, he scored centuries in three consecutive innings, albeit in different matches. Another surprise for so prolific an opener is that he never carried his bat. Robertson did, however, score more than a hundred runs on the first morning of a match on three occasions – a Middlesex record. The unlucky victims were Warwickshire at Lord's

in 1939, Nottinghamshire at Trent Bridge in 1947 and Sussex at Lord's in 1957.

Robertson was involved in a number of high stands, the best being 310 with Syd Brown against Nottinghamshire at Lord's in 1947. It was to remain a first-wicket record for Middlesex for 20 years. The pair were involved in 2 other double-century opening stands in that glad season, and a further 2 in subsequent seasons. Against Somerset at Lord's in 1951, the pair added 199 and 109 for the first wicket.

Not renowned for his fielding, Robertson nevertheless held 301 catches, to put him high on the Middlesex list. One imagines he was as undemonstrative here as in his batting.

Jack Robertson was desperately unlucky to have won only 11 Test caps. His record was 881 runs (46.36), most admittedly against 'lesser' teams. In later years he expressed disappointment, but never bitterness. It was not his nature.

In 1960, Robertson became Middlesex coach. He also became a popular guest at 'Cricket Societies' with his taped recordings of talks with old Middlesex stalwarts. As always he showed himself to be a true cricket gentleman.

Robert Walter Vivian Robins
RHB, LBG, 1925-1951

Born: 3 June 1906, Stafford
Died: 12 December 1968, Marylebone

Batting

M	I	NO	Runs	Av
258	378	24	9337	26.37

50	100	ct/st
50	6	142

Bowling

Balls	Runs	Wkts	Av	5wl	10wM
29288	14907	669	22.28	38	2

Best Performances
140 v. Cambridge at Fenner's, 1930
8-69 v. Gloucestershire at Lord's, 1929

Walter Robins was one of the most dynamic of all cricketers, positive and aggressive both on and off the field, who used up much nervous energy, was intolerant of excuses or faint-heartedness and if the results on the field were not always as desired, he kept the spectators entertained and interested.

Robins' batting, even as a Highgate schoolboy, was always busy, brisk and antagonistic towards the opposition. He used his feet, lifted and swung his bat, scored runs in a variety of places, or got out. Likewise, his bowling was sometimes erratic in length and direction, but always likely to get wickets, sometimes with the most unlikely balls. As a cover fielder, Robins always set the best of examples. Robins was county captain from 1935 to 1938 and again in 1946/47. His team achieved one title, 4 seconds and a third, a fine record under any circumstances. He returned aged forty-three in 1950 and the results were disastrous. Another old player not recognising that he and the times had changed? Sadly, this seems likely and it was a most inappropriate end to a distinguished playing career.

Given that he was an amateur with a career outside cricket, Robins' total of 258 appearances is creditable and he is one of only 10 players to exceed 5,000 runs and 500 wickets for Middlesex. The highest of his 6 centuries was 140 in 165 minutes, at Cambridge in 1930, by far the best batting in a match Middlesex lost abjectly. His best championship innings was 137 in only 119 minutes against Sussex at Lord's in 1938. He then proceeded to take 6 for 69, Sussex lost by an innings and Robins had certainly played a captain's part. He frequently led from the front: his 129 and 5 for 53 against Nottinghamshire at Trent Bridge in 1946 helped materially towards an innings win, while 102 in 90 minutes and a fifth-wicket stand of 171 with Alec Thompson set Middlesex on the victory road against Essex at Lord's at the end of the same season. A quickfire double of 101 and 74 against Kent at Dover in 1948 had seen Middlesex to victory

The veteran Robins shows he still means business.

after other batsmen had pottered around in a manner which must have disappointed their skipper (to put it mildly). 1946 saw some consistent batting and his only 1,000-run season, but Robins would not measure success this way. He did not compile runs, he won matches.

Similarly he only had one 100-wicket season – in 1929 – and his best bowling analysis, 8 for 69, came against Gloucs at Lord's (surprisingly in a losing cause) that season. His 7 for 36 against Hants at Lord's in 1933 saw his side win, as also his 7-77, same opposition and venue in 1938. His match figures of 11 for 99 certainly took care of Cambridge in 1946. Against Leicestershire at Lord's in 1929 he performed a hat-trick as Middlesex won narrowly on a rain-affected pitch.

Robins was patently a match-decisive performer with bat or ball, yet strangely rarely excelled in both facets in the same match. Had he done this he would have been a truly great all-rounder.

In Test matches Robins played 19 times, and was skipper thrice. 612 runs (26.60), 1 century, 12 catches and 64 wickets (27.46) suggest a player slightly below top class. He was a Cambridge Blue 1926-28 and in 1929 played in sufficient non-county matches to perform the 'double'. As Test selector 1946–48 and 1962–64, his teams were not always successful, though as manager of MCC in West Indies in 1959/60 he oversaw a series win which surprised many. In later years, however, he had become ever more cantankerous and impatient – possibly symptomatic of the onset of the lengthy and distressing illness which caused his early death – and by 1964 his time was done.

Michael Anthony Roseberry
RHB, 1986-2001

Born: 28 November 1966, Sunderland, Co. Durham

Batting

M	I	NO	Runs	Av
189	315	37	10010	36.00
157	150	12	4207	30.48

50	100	ct/st
49	20	135
29	4	52

Bowling

Balls	Runs	Wkts	Av	5wI	10wM
477	387	4	96.75	-	-
36	51	1	-	-	-

Best Performances
185 v. Leicestershire at Lord's, 1993
112 v. Shropshire at Telford, 1992

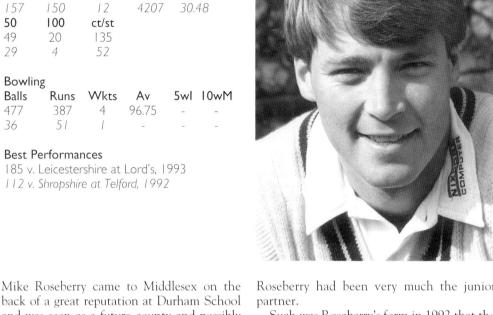

Mike Roseberry came to Middlesex on the back of a great reputation at Durham School and was seen as a future county and possibly England captain. He certainly never lived up to such high hopes but for several years was a confident and powerful batsman, with the ability to score heavily.

Four times, between 1990 and 1994, Roseberry exceeded 1,000 runs in a season, and in 1992 he reached a most impressive peak, with 2,044, average 56.67, and 9 centuries. To his orignal power and self-confidence was added a maturity which suggested a full England place was imminent. Roseberry scored 9 centuries in this season, the best individual tally for Middlesex since the great season of 1947. The highest was perhaps the most significant – an epic 6-hour 173 against his native Durham at Lord's in July. Against Nottinghamshire at Trent Bridge, Roseberry (148) outscored Desmond Haynes in a first-wicket stand of 266. Two years earlier, the two had added 306 for the first wicket against Essex at Ilford, when

Roseberry had been very much the junior partner.

Such was Roseberry's form in 1992 that the top echelons seemed to beckon but he suffered a bad slump in 1993 and although some improvement was shown in 1994 he was rarely at his known best and it was no great surprise when he left at the season's end to take over the Durham captaincy.

What seemed like a good move to resurrect a career which had gone stale turned out to be a personal disaster. The Durham captaincy weighed on him heavily, his strokeplay became inhibited and circumspect, due in some measure to his suspicions of his home pitches, and his form was almost unbelievably bad.

More hope than expectation accompanied Roseberry's return to Middlesex in 1999 and, as so often happens, going back did not work. After three indifferent seasons, he finally retired in 2001. A final career record for all first-class cricket of 11,950 runs, average 33.37, looks reasonably acceptable, but so much more was expected.

William Eric Russell

RHB, OB, 1956-1972

Born: 3 July 1936, Dumbarton, Scotland

Batting

M	I	NO	Runs	Av
400	712	54	23103	35.11
57	56	4	1386	26.65

50	100	ct/st
126	37	274
9	1	22

Bowling

Balls	Runs	Wkts	Av	5wI	10wM
1163	643	10	64.30	-	-
12	9	0	-	-	-

Best Performances

193 v. Hampshire at Bournemouth, 1964
123 v. Surrey at Lord's, 1968
2-46 v. Pakistanis at Lord's, 1962

Scots-born Eric Russell was a tall and always stylish batsman with an upright and fluent style who promised a great deal early in his career but perhaps never quite achieved the international renown some thought he should and could have done. For Middlesex, however, he was a splendid servant, who in his seemingly quiet way did much to bolster a struggling side.

Russell is the 7th most prolific Middlesex scorer of all time, beaten only by Jack Robertson as a regular opener. In exceeding 1,000 runs in 13 seasons he is beaten by only 7 other Middlesex players, while among openers only Jack Robertson, again, has achieved more than his 1,000 runs in 13 seasons consecutively. Russell reached his peak in 1964; his 2,342 runs (av. 45.92) is beaten by only 5 other batsmen for the county.

Russell obtained 37 centuries for Middlesex yet no-one has scored so many runs for the county without a double century. His best score was 193 on the first day of the Hampshire game at Bournemouth in 1964. He batted for 330 minutes and according to *Wisden* he drove and pulled superbly. One of Russell's best innings came that same season, when against Lancashire he scored 158 in 5 hours, and no-one else on either side exceeded 32. That Middlesex won by an innings was due almost wholly to Russell's batting. Perhaps Russell's most memorable innings, however, was his 167 against Pakistan at Lord's in 1967, when he and Michael Harris broke the then first-wicket record, adding 312 in less than 5 hours. It was perhaps symptomatic of Russell's demeanour that Harris received more acclaim yet Russell scored more quickly and heavily.

Russell's overall record for Middlesex, though certainly very impressive suggested when examined more closely that he was more led than leading. If the team played well in a season so did he. Likewise in opposite circumstances.

In 10 Test matches, Eric Russell scored 362 rins, average 21.29. He never really threatened to gain a regular place despite his methods suggesting otherwise.

Stanley Winckworth Scott
RHB, RF, 1878-1893

Born: 24 March 1854, Bombay, India
Died: 8 December 1933, Beckenham, Kent

Batting

M	I	NO	Runs	Av
97	178	18	3798	26.10
50	100	ct/st		
21	1	60		

Bowling

Balls	Runs	Wkts	Av	5wl	10wM
455	199	3	66.33	-	-

Best Performances

224 v. Gloucestershire at Lord's, 1892
1-20 v. Surrey at The Oval, 1878

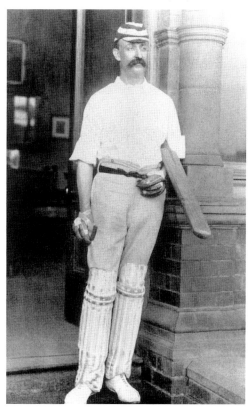

Stanley Winckworth Scott, powerful of build and with a distinctively profuse dark moustache, was strong in defence and possessed a range of orthodox front of the wicket off-side strokes. He matured late, but was a valuable batsman when able to play.

Scott's best season was undoubtedly 1892, when he scored 861 runs, average 39.13, for the county. Exceeding 1,000 runs in all first-class cricket, and playing for the Gentlemen, he was selected as a *Wisden* cricketer of the year. He enjoyed a golden spell of 629 runs in 9 completed innings, which included his best score and final Middlesex century, 224 against Gloucestershire at Lord's. He is reported to have batted 400 minutes and hit 22 fours and he set his side up for an innings victory. He played usefully in 1893 but then with business claims pressing was seen no more.

Scott's first century had come against Surrey at The Oval in 1882 when he dominated a stand of 102 with Alexander Webbe; Scott's 126 almost brought an unlikely win.

Perhaps a finer innings was the unbeaten 135 against Gloucestershire at Lord's in 1885 when he batted only 175 minutes. Sadly for Middlesex, and Scott, they lost by 8 wickets after a good first-innings lead. His 121 not out against Kent at Lord's in 1888 was also in a losing cause. The evidence suggests that here was a true back-to-the-wall, stiff-upper-lip type of batsman who relished a fight when all around him were failing.

Scott, a son of the Raj, spread his talents around profusely and once scored 138 for Herefordshire while visiting the county. He also played for many different clubs, mainly in the south, and earned his living in banking and subsequently on the Stock Exchange. Had he had the time, and ambition, he could well have possessed the characteristics to have taken on the Australians in Test matches – possibly even as captain.

Michael Walter William Selvey ——————— 100

RHB, RFM, 1972-1982

Born: 25 April 1948, Chiswick

Batting

M	I	NO	Runs	Av
213	212	65	1835	12.48
226	116	45	709	9.98
50	100	ct/st		
3	-	56		
-	-	39		

Bowling

Balls	Runs	Wkts	Av	5wI	10wM
34069	15653	615	25.45	33	3
10884	6147	290	21.19	2	-

Best Performances

67 v. Zimbabwe XI at Bulawayo, 1980-81
38* v. Essex at Chelmsford, 1979
7-20 v. Gloucestershire at Gloucester, 1976
5-18 v. Glamorgan at Cardiff, 1975

Mike Selvey, who first made a name for himself as a London schools representative, was tallish with a high action which enabled him to obtain lift from most surfaces. He also swung the ball both ways (though not at the same time – that would have made him unplayable) and in the right weather conditions (damp with heavy cloud), he could be devastating. Selvey had in fact played for Surrey, with limited success, in his youth and won a Blue at Cambridge, while late in his career he had a spell of modest success as Glamorgan captain. It was as a Middlesex support seamer that he made his name and was chosen for three Test matches. He began his Test career like the proverbial 'house on fire' but quickly faded into insignificance.

For Middlesex, Selvey gave fine service and in an era when the feat was becoming rarer and more difficult, once took 100 wickets in a season. 101 wickets, average 19.09 was his return, 1978 the year, and it is highly unlikely any paceman will ever again match this achievement for the county.

Selvey's best figures for Middlesex came against Gloucestershire at Gloucester in 1976, when his 7 for 20 in indifferent light put the skids under the home county and played a material part in an innings win for the visitors. This effort had come shortly after match-winning figures of 11 for 112 against Oxford University and such form must have counted greatly in his favour with the Test selectors, who chose him for his Test debut in the same season.

Selvey's performances never really reached such heights again but for several years he was an integral part of one of the most successful spells ever enjoyed by the county. It also helped that although hardly an all-rounder he sometimes showed more batting ability than the average tailender and was a deep thinker about the game.

This latter quality has been reflected in a successful post-playing career as journalist and radio pundit. An appreciation of the works of John Betjeman also probably stands him in good stead.

Owais Alam Shah
RHB, OB, 1996 to date

Born: 22 October 1978, Karachi, Pakistan

Batting
M	I	NO	Runs	Av
91	150	11	4988	35.88
122	*114*	*13*	*2922*	*28.93*

50	100	ct/st
24	12	54
13	*4*	*35*

Bowling
Balls	Runs	Wkts	Av	5wI	10wM
996	627	17	36.88	-	-
231	*249*	*8*	*31.12*	-	-

Best Performances
203 v. Derbyshire at Southgate, 2001
134 v. Sussex at Arundel, 1999
3-33 v. Gloucestershire at Bristol, 1999
2-2 v. Glamorgan at Cardiff, 1998

The arrival of Owais Shah in 1996 was looked upon with considerable excitement since he had already established a reputation in schools cricket. The following season he came into the side on completion of his A-levels and the penultimate game, against Nottinghamshire at Lord's, saw him obtain his maiden century. Aged 18 years 234 days, he was the youngest century scorer for the county since Denis Compton.

The signs were surely propitious but in the next two seasons he seemed to mark time somewhat. The neat technique and style remained but he failed to become the heavy scorer hoped for. There was manifest difficulty in trying to make his way in a struggling side but there is also evidence that for whatever reason some of his supporters – and there were many – seemed satisfied with under-achievement from their protégé.

The 2000 season actually saw a marked regression in form with fewer than 500 first-class runs but happily in 2001, for the first time, he showed signs of an ability to score big runs, reaching 1,000 runs for the county for the first time. Among his 3 first-class centuries were a superb 203 in 461 minutes against Derbyshire at Southgate, and this remains as his best score. Earlier in the season he had scored 190 and 88 against Durham at Chester-le-Street and a few weeks after his double century came a stylish 144 against Nottinghamshire at Trent Bridge. Unfortunately, between times and subsequently, Shah achieved little, so 1,040 runs at 41.60 looks misleadingly good. In 2002, he had another 1,000-run season and a slightly improved average. It was a season of large scoring by his county, on good wickets against often poor bowling and his team, thankfully for its supporters, won promotion.

2003, against better county attacks, could be vital for the stylist whose smooth stroke play so impressed as a teenager. He has played a handful of limited-overs international matches, but failed to establish himself. In his twenty-fifth year, Test status seems almost as remote as ever and he is no longer in the first flush of youth.

Harry Philip Hugh Sharp

RHB, RM, OB, 1946-1955

Born: 6 October 1917, Kentish Town, London

Died: 15 January 1995, Enfield

Batting

M	I	NO	Runs	Av
162	266	28	6141	25.80
50	100	ct/st		
30	9	59		

Bowling

Balls	Runs	Wkts	Av	5wI	10wM
3489	1628	50	32.56	1	-

Best Performances

165 v. Northamptonshire at Northampton, 1951

5-52 v. Oxford University at Oxford, 1949

Harry Sharp was the type of cricketer who sadly, no longer exists. He joined the Lord's staff as a teenager and remained there for the whole of his normal working life and far beyond, into his mid-seventies. All the time he was known (and loved) as a genial good-humoured easy-going type, happy with a drink and a cigarette after the day's play, and the best friend to any young player needing comfort or solace, or simply a drinking partner.

Sharp probably lost vital years to the war, when he was involved in more important business in the Royal Navy, but although he was in his twenty-nineth year before making his first-class debut he remained a valuable part of the Middlesex playing set-up for ten years.

Sharp's usual batting style has elsewhere been described as 'dour' and usually he seemed content to plod along at his own pace, leaving aggression to others more accomplished in the art. There were times, however, as he liked to point out, when he too put some strokes together. For example, against Derbyshire at Lord's in 1953 he wended his way to his half century in his normal steady manner and then

raced to his century in a further 35 minutes. There were other occasions when the situation decreed, or simply when the spirit was with him, that he showed his array of strokes. At Cheltenham in 1947 for instance, on a turning wicket, Sharp set about Tom Goddard, hitting him for 8 leg-side fours in his vital 46, and then shared the fourth-innings bowling spoils with Sims and Young to seal a victory which effectively gave Middlesex the title. Ever afterwards, Sharp relished visits to Cheltenham.

Harry Sharp three times exceeded 1,000 runs in a season, his best return coming in 1953 when he scored 1,424 runs, average 31.00. He scored 4 centuries that season and sometimes showed unwonted aggression, yet it is probable the innings which gave him most satisfaction in 1953 was 103 in five hours on a Derby greentop against Gladwin and Jackson. Harry seemed to rest content with that. He never scored another first-class hundred and his career, from that point, went into gentle decline.

Sharp scored 9 centuries altogether for the county and the highest was 165 against Northamptonshire at Northampton in 1951.

Harry Sharp (left) looks on as Len Muncer bowls at Lord's in 1952.

He drove strongly for more than 5 hours. In a match with much fine batting and an exciting albeit inconclusive result, Harry was the cement around which the Middlesex challenge was built.

No more than an occasional opener for most of his career, Sharp was nevertheless involved in two first-wicket stands of more than 200, both with Syd Brown, as deputy for Jack Robertson. Against Cambridge in 1949 they put on 229, Sharp being dismissed for 98 which *Wisden* reckoned would have been a century had they run better between the wickets. Next season against Worcestershire at Lord's, the pair put on 227 on the first day in a match Middlesex won easily.

Sharp did occasional good work with medium-paced off spin and against Oxford in 1949 had figures of 5 for 52. His fielding was little remarked upon; doubtless he went where he was ordered and did his best.

After giving up playing, Harry Sharp was a coach at Lord's for a number of years and from 1972 to 1993 he was scorer for Middlesex, a job he performed without ostentation and which he quietly relinquished when computerisation was introduced. He was aged seventy-five; the time was right.

Harry Sharp continued his interest in cricket and the other established facets of his life. The day he died he had been for a pie and a pint; perhaps there was a betting slip in his pocket. What a way to go for a man so much part of the Middlesex scene that county supporters at away matches were known to arrive and check the scorebox. 'Ah yes, Harry's there'. God was in his Heaven, all was right with the world.

James Morton Sims

RHB, LBG, 1929-1952

Born: 13 May 1903, Leyton, Essex
Died: 27 April 1973, Canterbury, Kent

Batting

M	I	NO	Runs	Av
381	515	96	7173	17.11
50	100	ct/st		
18	3	202		

Bowling

Balls	Runs	Wkts	Av	5wI	10wM
60512	31708	1257	25.22	77	14

Best Performances

121 v. Northamptonshire at Kettering, 1937
9-92 v. Lancashire at Old Trafford, 1934

Jim Sims' doleful expression masked an East London sense of humour, a gift for mimicry and an ability to leg-pull not appreciated by one internationally famous fast bowler and cricket personality convinced that Sims had spent his youth in the 'Leyton coalfield'. Sims was also a cricketer of high talent, who started out as a batsman of possibilities and became a bowler of leg spin with unusually good control and a well-concealed googly.

Sims was twenty-six before making his debut, twenty-nine when he received his cap. Since he did most things late it is hardly surprising that his last first-class match for the county was against the 1952 Indian team, when he was forty-nine, and he was still a regular aged forty-eight.

Sims's best season was 1939, when he took 143 wickets, average 25.55. He also exceeded 100 wickets in 1935, 1947 and 1949, when a lot of dusty pitches saw a resurgence in his form. In other seasons he came pretty close to the century.

Although Sims' best analysis in all first-class cricket was 10-90 for The East v. The West at the 1948 Kingston festival (he was a remarkable forty-five years old, and had been intending to retire) his best for the county was a probably more notable 9 for 92 against Lancashire at Old Trafford in 1934. Lancashire were then top of the championship table, their batting was very strong and they did win the match. But Sims, with barely any support, bowled magnificently for 34.1 overs, and finished with a spell of 5 for 6 in 22 balls, and 3 for 0 in the last 5. The following season, when he took 100 wickets for the first time, he enjoyed a lethal run from 24 to 29 July. When Middlesex beat Hampshire at Lord's, Sims followed first innings figures of 8 for 84 in 41.4 overs with 3 for 43 and then he had match figures of 13 for 91 as Essex were beaten in 2 days at Ilford. He then went down to Taunton and enjoyed match figures of 9 for 125 in another Middlesex win. Sims had some fine performances in his golden summer of

1939. As war clouds were gathering, he destroyed Derbyshire on their own midden with match figures of 13 for 132. Earlier in the season, he had performed similar torture at Northampton. His figures were 12 for 224 as the home team laid down their arms to him.

Despite aging fingers which suffered in the cold, 1948 saw a number of fine performances. Against Leicestershire at Leicester, match figures of 11 for 122 (when best support came from the Irishman, Eddie Ingram) were instrumental in a 10-wicket win while near the end, Surrey collapsed to an innings defeat at headquarters, due mainly to centuries from Brown and Compton, and 10 for 122 from Jim Sims. The following season, Leicestershire succumbed on their home ground and the forty-six-year-old Sims swept them away with 10 for 177 in the match, and second innings figures of 7 for 38 in 10.3 overs. The theory that spinners improve with age has been discredited but Sims seemed to be aiming to damn those more bothered with fact than romance.

Sims started mainly as a batsman and did in fact hit 3 hundreds. The highest was the best: 121 against Northamptonshire at Kettering in 1937 scored in the last 85 minutes of the first day. He and Len Muncer added 135 in 55 minutes for the eighth wicket. It was hectic and demoralising stuff.

When finally having to bow to the inevitable and stop playing he became county coach and then scorer, dying in harness after collapsing at a Canterbury Hotel during a pre-season friendly.

Jim Sims' Test record is 4 Test matches, 16 runs and 11 wickets. Sims' expression might have looked the part for Test cricket, but in fact it was perhaps too serious a business for him.

Jim Sims in a typically doleful pose.

Wilfred Norris Slack

LHB, RM, 1977-1988

Born: 12 December 1954, Troumaca, St Vincent

Died: 15 January 1989, Banjul, The Gambia

Batting

M	I	NO	Runs	Av
210	348	38	12565	40.53
165	157	18	4075	29.31

50	100	ct/st
66	25	146
28	2	32

Bowling

Balls	Runs	Wkts	Av	5wI	10wM
1380	632	19	33.26	-	-
1606	1229	42	29.26	1	-

Best Performances

248* v. Worcestershire at Lord's, 1981
110 v. Somerset at Lord's, 1987
3-17 v. Leicestershire at Uxbridge, 1982
5-32 v. Leicestershire at Lord's, 1983

Wilf Slack was a heavy scorer who usually relied more on application and sound technique than dazzling stroke play, but he was no less valuable for that, and thoroughly deserved his trial in the England Test team. He made little impact, but for a man in his thirties it was a little late for him.

For his county, Slack, who came to Middlesex from Buckinghamshire, exceeded 1,000 runs in 8 successive seasons, including his last. His best season's tally was 1,899 (av. 54.25) in 1985. As a prolific scorer, Slack stands 18th among Middlesex players but in averaging more than 40 he is 8th among those with any sort of career for the county.

Slack was self-evidently a scorer of 'big tons', as his three double centuries for the county confirm. His highest was an epic 248* against Worcestershire at Lord's in 1981. The following season, he hit 203* against Oxford and against the 1985 Australians scored 201* in 530 minutes for the best score in Middlesex/Australia matches.

Wilf Slack twice carried his bat throughout an innings: 72 out of 195 v. Worcestershire at Lord's in 1985 and 152 out of 252 v. Yorkshire at Headingley the following season. His last two centuries, 163* and 105*, were scored in the same match v. Glamorgan in 1988.

Against Kent at Lord's in 1981 Slack and Barlow added 367 for the first wicket, at the time a county record and still the best unbroken opening stand. He and Barlow also put on 225 against Surrey at The Oval in 1985; with John Carr he added 221 against Surrey in 1987.

Wilf Slack seemed to have plenty of runs left in him, and a future coaching job beckoning, perhaps with disadvantaged youngsters, when he collapsed and died at the wicket in the Gambia in January 1989. Slack had suffered blackouts for some time, but it was a horrendous shock for all those who had so admired a modest and talented man, who died trying to pass on his enjoyment of what he did best. His memory remains vivid in 2003.

Cedric Ivan James Smith
RHB, RF, 1934-1939

Born: 25 August 1906, Corsham, Wiltshire
Died: 9 February 1979, Mellor, Lancashire

Batting

M	I	NO	Runs	Av
152	216	23	2977	15.42
50	**100**	**ct/st**		
10	1	69		

Bowling

Balls	Runs	Wkts	Av	5wI	10wM
33078	12001	676	17.75	39	8

Best Performances
101* v. Kent at Canterbury, 1939
8-102 v. Hampshire at Southampton, 1934

The misused phrase 'a legend in his own life-time' could certainly be applied to Jim Smith, 6ft 4in tall and massively built. He used his physical assets to make himself one of the hardest hitters of a cricket ball of all time. Smith reputedly possessed only one 'stroke', the aim of which was to plant the ball among the leg-side spectators. Smith was also an excellent fast bowler: pacey, accurate and with lift and stamina.

Jim Smith was in his twenty-eighth year when he started his Middlesex career. He had played for his native Wiltshire for a number of years and unfortunately for Smith, a mix-up over his registration meant that his first-class career was put on hold for two years. Smith quickly made up for lost time. After a slowish start Smith finished that first season, 1934, with 143 wickets, average 17.52, and no other Middlesex bowler has had such a debut season, either before or since. Smith really hit form in late May with first innings figures of 7 for 107 (11-201 the match) and in the next game at Southampton he shattered Hampshire with first innings figures of 8 for 104. This was to remain his best analysis for the whole of his career but the dire support offered him saw Middlesex lose. Middlesex then returned to Lord's and Smith destroyed a weak Northamptonshire batting line-up with match figures of 10 for 50. If Jim Smith never again showed the consistent effectiveness of his first season, in four seasons of his short six-season career he exceeded 100 wickets, his return of 136, average 15.94, in 1937 being especially impressive. Perhaps the best performance of his career occurred this season, when after being set only 100 for victory Nottinghamshire lost 7 wickets for 57, all to Smith before he tired and they limped home.

Jim Smith left it until August 1939, as war clouds were gathering, to record his only first-class century. Going in at number 10 against Kent at Canterbury he scored 101* out of 121 in 81 minutes, hitting 7 sixes, and helped Peebles (14) add 116 for the tenth wicket. Even more explosive was his 66 in 18 minutes against Gloucestershire in 1938; he reached 50 in 11 minutes, the fastest, genuine half century ever.

Michael John Smith ———————————————

RHB, SLA, 1959-1980

Born: 4 January 1942, Enfield

Batting

M	I	NO	Runs	Av
399	664	77	18575	31.64
219	216	4	5775	27.24

50	100	ct/st
82	37	210
30	4	173

Bowling

Balls	Runs	Wkts	Av	5wI	10wM
4082	1857	57	32.57	-	-
38	43	2	21.50	-	-

Best Performances

181 v. Lancashire at Old Trafford, 1967
123 v. Hampshire at Lord's, 1977
4-13 v. Gloucestershire at Lord's, 1961

Mike Smith started out as so promising a left-armed spinner, that he won awards for his exploits with the Enfield Grammar School and Public School Representative teams. It was for his promise as a bowler that he was taken on to the Middlesex staff, yet he was eventually to establish himself as a combative opening bat who did so well for his county that he won 5 limited-overs international caps for England and at his best was not far below Test quality.

Mike Smith obtained 37 first-class centuries for Middlesex, the highest being his second, 181 against Lancashire at Old Trafford in 1967, an innings described by *Wisden* as 'faultless'. Smith was a very smooth operator when in his best form, as is indicated by his first-morning century against Kent at Canterbury in 1974, when he dominated an opening stand of 169 with Brearley. He had shown similar enterprise when racing to 100* before lunch on the second morning of the away Leicestershire match in 1973 and he also made an early effort to go for victory in the second innings before the loss of several partners saw the run race abandoned.

Although suffering occasional dips in form, Smith exceeded 1,000 runs in 10 seasons with a best of 1,705, average 39.65, in 1970, and is the 13th most prolific rungetter in Middlesex history. Curiously, for so prolific an opener, Smith was involved in only one first-wicket stand of more than 200, against Sussex at Hove in 1970 when he and Eric Russell added 209 after Middlesex were forced to follow on, thus converting a near-certain defeat into a draw with Sussex hanging on for their lives.

After retirement, Smith, whose 399 appearances place him 12th on the all-time Middlesex list, was employed by Ealing Council but he subsequently succeeded Harry Sharp as scorer; after early problems it is a job he now does well and conscientiously.

Greville Thomas Scott Stevens

RHB, LB, 1919-1932

Born: 7 January 1901, Hampstead
Died: 19 September 1970, Islington, London

Batting

M	I	NO	Runs	Av
127	195	15	5434	30.18

50	100	ct/st
32	7	107

Bowling

Balls	Runs	Wkts	Av	5wI	10wM
18927	10556	385	27.41	15	3

Best Performances

170* v. Warwickshire at Edgbaston, 1931
8-38 v. Hampshire at Portsmouth, 1922

Tall and good looking, Stevens established himself as a cricketer to be reckoned with while still at UCS, scoring 466 in a single innings of a house match there in 1919. He was also a lethal leg-break bowler and was accorded the honour of selection for the Gentlemen against The Players at Lord's that season. He gained his Blue at Oxford and led the side in 1922, but after going down his work on the Stock Exchange precluded regular appearances for Middlesex and he never really attained the heights once predicted.

Though he never scored 1,000 runs or took 100 wickets in a season, Stevens still performed well for the county. His best batting season was 1931 when he scored 939 runs and obtained 3 centuries, including his career best, 170* against the weak Warwickshire attack at Edgbaston, he and Hendren adding 218 quickfire runs for the third wicket. A few weeks later, Stevens scored 117 against the same side at Lord's, when he and Tim Killick added 277, at that time the highest opening stand for any county at Lord's and still the best for Middlesex against Warwickshire.

As with many top spinners, much of Stevens' most lethal bowling came early in his career. His best innings analysis came against Hampshire at Portsmouth in 1922. He took 8 for 38 in 17.2 overs and a Hampshire performance regarded at the time as abject. It was against Hampshire at Lord's at Whitsun in 1919 that the schoolboy Stevens made his first-class debut, having 7 for 104 in his first innings and 10 for 136 in the match.

Stevens' 10 Test appearances brought ordinary career figures and it could be said that neither his batting, owing much to powerful forearms and watchfulness, or his bowling, which exhibited great power of spin but at times poor control, improved much. He lacked regular pactice, and had a living to earn. However 10,376 runs (av. 29.56), 213 catches and 684 wickets (av. 26.84) in all first-class cricket was a good record.

RHB, RM, 1885-1900

Born: 11 March 1863, Westoe, South Shields, Co. Durham
Died: 4 April 1915, St John's Wood

Batting

M	I	NO	Runs	Av
170	300	9	9255	31.80
50	**100**	**ct/st**		
39	16	156		

Bowling

Balls	Runs	Wkts	Av	5wI	10wM
8827	4038	141	28.63	2	-

Best Performances
221 v. Somerset at Lord's, 1900
5-78 v. Surrey at Lord's, 1896

'Drewey' Stoddart, who as with many great and successful sportsmen had family origins in the North East, first found fame in 1886 when scoring 485 in an innings (at the time the highest ever in any form of cricket) for Hampstead against The Stoics. He subsequently became one of the most distinguished amateur batsmen of his day and captain of England. Although not starting serious cricket until his twenties, Stoddart was a superb opening bat, sound in defence but with an array of attacking strokes, with his dominant bottom hand ensuring on side bias. He was also a serviceable bowler and versatile fielder.

Stoddart's 215* against Lancashire at Old Trafford in 1891 was the first championship double century for Middlesex, a marvellous 5-hour knock (the next best score was 51) in which he was the backbone of an innings win. It is still the best score in Middlesex/Lancashire matches. Stoddart's own best score, 221 against Somerset at Lord's was even more remarkable. He was in for less than 5 hours and hit 36 fours. Amazingly he only played out of respect for the beneficiery J.T.

Hearne. It was his only match of the season, and his last ever for Middlesex. Another remarkable performance came against Notts at Lord's in 1893. He raced to 101* by lunch on the first day, eventually carrying his bat for 195 out of 327, and in the second innings scored a brilliant 124. Stoddart's batting alone ensured a narrow victory.

Stoddart exceeded 1,000 runs three times. Unremarkable? Perhaps, but when he achieved the feat for a third time in 1898, no-one else had done it even once. His best season's total was 1,178, average 47.12, in 1893, an average and tally of runs more than half as much again as anyone else.

When Stoddart and T.C. O'Brien added 228 for the first wicket after following on against Surrey at The Oval in 1893 it was a Middlesex first-wicket record which set their side on the road to an unexpected victory. The only previous double-century stand for this wicket had been by Stoddart and Alexander Webbe, 205 v. Kent at Gravesend in 1886, when Stoddart scored his maiden century. The next was 218 against Yorkshire

in 1896. The partners were Herbert Hayman and, of course, A.E. Stoddart.

Throughout his Middlesex career, Stoddart had a reputation for playing match-decisive innings and for unselfishness on the field. This was recognised when he skippered England on 8 occasions and in his first series regained the Ashes in one of the most exciting of Test rubbers.

Stoddart was a marvellous all-round sportsman; he won 10 caps for England at rugby football and skippered the team. He was also a topline performer at lawn tennis, rackets and squash – anything, it seemed, with a moving ball requiring quickness of eye and co-ordination.

Stoddart was one of a number of cricketers to take his own life. Shortly after resigning as secretary of the Queen's (Lawn Tennis) Club he shot himself through the head at home. He was suffering from bad health and financial worries, and it was found that he was in the initial stages of pneumonia, which would have increased his depression. He had also endured an arid and childless marriage. Thus came the saddest of ends for a great cricketer once immortalised in verse as 'My dear Victorious Stod'. The question has to be, as with so many successful people in decline, when was the exact time things started to go wrong? The 'Rosebud' element, if you like.

Andrew John Strauss

LHB, LM, 1998 to date

Born: 2 March 1977, Johannesburg, S. Africa

Batting

M	I	NO	Runs	Av
62	104	5	3840	38.78
67	63	3	1385	23.08
50	100	ct/st		
19	7	35		
10	-	13		

Bowling

Balls	Runs	Wkts	Av	5wI	10wM
12	16	0	-	-	-

Best Performances

176 v. Durham at Lord's, 2001
90 v. Durham at Chester-le-Street, 2000

It is on players such as Andrew Strauss that the fortunes of Middlesex and even England cricket will depend, not only as a batsman whose technique seems so eminently sound that his future at the top of the order in the very highest class of cricket would appear to be assured, but also as an apparently natural captain.

Strauss made his debut against Hampshire at Southampton in late 1998, after being a member of the successful Durham University side in the BUSA competition. He immediately gave notice that he was a batsman of both grace and determination, with the potential to reach the very top echelons of the game with his side's top score, 83. Strauss' progress during the following two seasons was rather more steady than spectacular.

His maiden century came in the opening match of the 2000 season – a comparatively staid unbeaten 111 against Northamptonshire at Lord's which enabled his skipper to declare in what was subsequently seen as an ambitious attempt to force a result. Strauss had done his job, however, and it was perhaps slightly disappointing for both player and team that although he averaged over 30 for the season only three more half centuries accrued.

2001 saw Strauss bat his way to the forefront of Middlesex cricket. The departure of Ramprakash and the Australian Langer, meant that a lot of runs had to be found from elsewhere and Strauss responded with 1,211 runs at 44.85, with 3 centuries. There were also such performances as a career best 176 in over 6 hours against Durham, and a fine double of 56 and 112* against Hampshire at Southampton at the season's end, when Strauss' batting stood out in an otherwise diabolical performance by a side supposedly going hard for promotion.

Another four-figure total in 2002, with 3 more centuries, sends Strauss and his admirers into 2003 and the Championship First Division with considerable optimism for the future. He has thus far sent the right messages.

Charles Thomas Studd
RHB, RM, 1879-1884

Born: 2 December 1860, Spratton, Northants.
Died: 16 July 1931, Ibambi, Belgian Congo
 (Republic of Congo)

Batting

M	I	NO	Runs	Av
34	54	10	1241	28.20
50	100	ct/st		
3	1	21		

Bowling

Balls	Runs	Wkts	Av	5wI	10wM
9875	3370	200	16.85	16	4

Best Performances
105* v. Kent at Canterbury, 1883
8-71 v. Gloucestershire at Cheltenham ,1882

Charles Studd was an all-rounder in the classical mould, tall and stylish as a batsman, with strokes to all parts although he favoured the off side, a bowler on the slowish side of medium who moved the ball either way from a high action, and a magnificent athletic fielder.

In a truncated Middlesex career he gave evidence of true international class; 1,241 runs and 200 wickets in 34 matches could hardly suggest otherwise. His only century for the county was an unbeaten 105 against Kent at Canterbury in 1883. In the same game he took 10 wickets for 124 (6 for 79 and 4 for 45), an all round effort which saw him win the match almost single handed. In the next match against Gloucestershire, he scored 91 and took 7 wickets towards an innings win. His bowling was superb for the county. In June 1882, he shattered Gloucestershire's second-innings resistance at Lord's with match-winning figures of 7 for 48; in the return at Cheltenham, Gloucestershire were even more under the cosh, Studd destroying them with second-innings figures of 8 for 71 and a match

return of 12 for 124. In 1883 at Lord's, he crushed Surrey with match figures of 10 for 140, then Yorkshire suffered 11 for 144, but held on for the draw. Against Kent at Lord's in 1884, he signed off his career with figures of 10 for 71 to win the game.

The future seemed assured; he had already played 5 Test matches and possibly revealed flaws in temperament. A dreadful performance by Studd in the 1882 Ashes Test match, when he seemed to abdicate responsibility, was much more to blame for the England defeat than the efforts of the usual culprit, the unfortunate Yorkshire professional, Peate.

Whether the faults would have been straightened out with experience will never be known. In 1885, he went to China as a missionary and devoted his life to spreading the Word firstly there, then in America and finally in the Belgian Congo, where he died. Manifestly he was a good man, yet when in the USA he never seemed to have bothered to visit brother George, also ex-Middlesex and England, in Los Angeles.

George Brown Studd

RHB, 1879-1886

Born: 20 October 1859, Netheravon, Wiltshire

Died: 13 February 1945, Pasadena, California

Batting

M	I	NO	Runs	Av
29	47	2	959	21.31
50	100	ct/st		
7	1	24		

Bowling

Balls	Runs	Wkts	Av	5wl	10wM
12	5	1	-	-	-

Best Performances

104 v. Kent at Lord's, 1885
1-5 v. Nottinghamshire at Trent Bridge, 1883

George Studd, older brother of Charles, played only 29 matches for Middlesex, the last before his twenty-seventh birthday, yet despite a mediocre record he was a stylish front-foot batter and a keen albeit erratic fielder who under other circumstances could have enjoyed a lengthy and distinguished cricket career.

George Studd was the second of several cricketing brothers, and one of three who skippered Cambridge. Interestingly, none of their direct descendants excelled at cricket but the 1939 Cambridge skipper, Peter Studd, was indirectly related.

Despite George Studd's experience at Cambridge (he was 4 years in the XI and when skipper in 1882, he played a magnificent four-hour 120, the best-ever score for an opening bat in the University match at that time), he took time to come to the fore with Middlesex. His form was badly affected by a broken arm in 1883/84, while his appearances were limited due to his being called to the Bar and it was not until 1885, when for non-cricketing reasons his career was already drawing to its close that he scored his first and only county century, some time after his brief Test career closed. He opened the batting against Kent at Lord's and hitting 104 in 165 minutes, he put Middlesex on the road to eventual victory. In 1886, he made only occasional appearances but against Gloucestershire at Gloucester in early August he scored 67, 'hitting with much brilliance' according to a contemporary report, and that was it. A first-class career record of 2,892 runs (av. 21.90) is little indeed to show for so talented a cricketer.

George Studd, of the hang-dog expression and dark eyes, had heard the same 'call' as brother Charlie. He worked in India and China and after 1891 in the United States. He appears to have lost touch with his family, Charles never visiting him when he too was in America. George seems to have given away everything he owned, living in penury, and dying in California of chronic malnutrition. Perhaps George Studd was the true Christian.

Francis Alfred Tarrant
RHB, SMLA, 1904-1914

Born: 11 December 1880, Fitzroy, Victoria, Australia
Died: 29 January 1951, Fitzroy

Batting

M	I	NO	Runs	Av
206	344	24	12169	38.02

50	100	ct/st		
55	26	193		

Bowling

Balls	Runs	Wkts	Av	5wI	10wM
43637	17518	1005	17.43	89	22

Best Performances
250* v. Essex at Leyton, 1914
9-41 v. Gloucestershire at Bristol, 1907

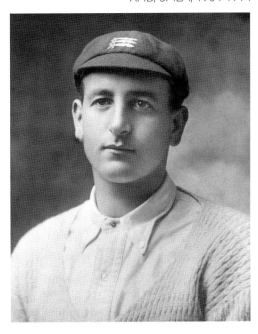

In so much as such a claim is reasonable and valid, Frank Tarrant is almost certainly the best cricketer not to appear in a Test match since the inception of the even-handed version of that style of cricket in 1877. As a batsman, he was usually very watchful but could vary his game according to need. He possessed an effective square cut and was also strong on the leg side. As a left-armed slow-medium bowler he tended to 'push it through' rather than flight and was lethal in favourable conditions. Contemporary descriptions suggest a strong similarity to Derek Underwood of Kent and England. Tarrant was also a safe field.

Tarrant came to England to qualify for Middlesex and his county career, curtailed by the First World War, was one long triumph. He scored 26 centuries for the county, 3 times going on to a double. His highest innings was a marvellous unbeaten 250 out of 464-1 declared in 320 minutes against Essex at Leyton in 1914. Middlesex won by an innings; Tarrant, who opened both batting and bowling, took 4 wickets. Tarrant and J.W. Hearne put on an unbroken 235 for the second wicket, and both scored more than 100 runs on the second morning. Good indeed, but dwarfed by the 380, the pair added for the same wicket against Lancashire at Lord's a few

weeks later. This remains a second-wicket record for the county. Tarrant scored 198 this time but a short while earlier he had scored exactly 200 against Worcestershire at Lord's; this time he and Hearne added 216 for the second wicket. Tarrant scored 1,743 runs, average 51.26, in this, his last county season. It was the 8th time he had reached 1,000, and the best.

Tarrant also had his best bowling season in 1914, with 131 wickets at 18.40. This was the 6th time he had exceeded 100 wickets, and each time he performed the 'double', a stupendous feat.

It is a minor miracle Tarrant never took an innings 'all-10' since he achieved 9 on five occasions, with 9 for 41 against Gloucestershire at Bristol in 1907 the statistical best. Tarrant recorded 12 for 132 in the match, had a spell of 4 wickets with consecutive balls and scored 98 in his only innings as Middlesex slaughtered the home team. Earlier in the season, Tarrant had 13 for 87 at Lord's against the same opposition. Tarrant had even better figures against Lancashire at Old Trafford in August 1914. He followed his first innings analysis of 9 for 105 with 7 for 71. After his match return of 16 for 176 he scored a brilliant, match-winning 101* in 2 hours. Perhaps an even more remarkable

bowling return was his 15 for 47 against Hampshire at Lord's in 1913. In 1914, Tarrant took 14 for 122 against Oxford while in 1908, he caught the Philadelphians on a treacherous wicket, recording match figures of 10 for 46 (and Albert Trott had 9 for 59). No wonder the Americans lost the urge to play cricket. There was also his 13 for 67 against Gloucestershire at Bristol in 1909, when he performed a hat-trick. Both these matches were over in a day, and manifestly played in poor conditions, yet Tarrant was the only batsman to reach a half century in the latter match, and second top scorer in the former.

Finally, Tarrant twice performed the match 'double' of a century and 10 wickets and his 6 catches in an innings against Essex at Leyton in 1906 is still equal best for Middlesex.

Just why did this stupendous all-rounder never play a Test? Well he left Australia before reaching his best but there was nothing in the contemporary rules which disqualified him from later playing for Australia, or alternatively qualifying for England. It is really a cricketing tragedy that this modest and talented all-rounder, who in later life made much money horse dealing, mainly in India, does not figure in Test records.

Alexander William Thompson
RHB, LB, 1939-1955

Born: 17 April 1916, Liverpool
Died: 13 January 2001, Illinois, United States

Batting

M	I	NO	Runs	Av
195	317	30	7641	26.62

50	100	ct/st
46	5	62

Bowling

Balls	Runs	Wkts	Av	5wI	10wM
1166	681	10	68.10	-	-

Best Performances
158 v. Worcestershire at Dudley, 1952
2-35 v. Oxford University at Oxford, 1953

Alexander Thompson was born on Merseyside but spent most of his formative years in North London and as with others the Second World War chipped a large piece out of his career-forming years.

Thompson took time to get going in 1946 but really came good in the eyes of the inhabitants of Highbury, his home state, with an unbeaten century against Surrey at The Oval. He and Walter Robins added a quickfire 148 in 80 minutes for the sixth wicket and Thompson reached his maiden century at the same time as making the winning hit. Perhaps Thompson never knew quite such glory again. It was 6 years before his second century. A fine unbeaten 140 against Yorkshire at Lord's in 1952 must have given special pleasure and this was followed by a career-best 158* against Worcestershire at the atmospheric Dudley ground. On this occasion, he opened the innings and added 315 with Bill Edrich for the second wicket. There was, in fact, always an indescribable (even Tolkienesque), wonderland charm about Thompson which was well suited to Dudley, a ground built over deep subterranean tunnels which in later years collapsed, taking most of the cricket field with them. Perhaps Thompson should have tried Worcestershire.

He followed with 109 against Lancashire at Old Trafford and 125 against Hampshire at Southampton in 1953, then it was back to the Second XI and retirement.

Thompson twice managed to score 1,000 runs in a season, his better total being 1,245 (av. 31.92) in 1953. In 1955, he was awarded a joint benefit with that other great servant Harry Sharp, and they each coined £7,427. This was the parting of the ways.

During his career, Thompson had established his credentials as one of the more unusual of professional cricketers by his interest in and knowledge of classical music. So, what did he do with his retirement? He emigrated to America and became a chemist in Illinois, of course. A full and proper biography of Alec Thompson would be of far more interest and moment than many others one could name.

Charles Inglis Thornton

RHB, RM underarm, 1975-1985

Born: 20 March 1850, Llanwarne,
Herefordshire
Died: 10 December 1929, Marylebone

Batting

M	I	NO	Runs	Av
29	48	1	883	18.78
50	100	ct/st		
4	-	14		

Bowling

Balls	Runs	Wkts	Av	5wI	10wM
96	32	1	-	-	-

Best Performances
79 v. Oxford University at Prince's, 1876

'Buns' Thornton was one of the biggest hitters ever to grace the first-class game amd a bowler of quick 'grub-hunters' which sometimes, though not for Middlesex, gained more than their just reward. Tall and strong, Thornton used his feet to get to the pitch and produced some of the longest drives and most powerful leg hits seen on any cricket field. For North v. South in 1871, it is claimed he made a hit off W.M. Rose measured at 152 yards, while in practice that same season he drove balls 168 yards 2 feet and 162 yards. In 1868, he drove balls over the pavilion at both Lord's and The Oval while at Canterbury he once hit Edward Walker out of the ground every ball of an over. During an innings of 107 in 80 minutes for the Gentlemen in 1886, he smote 7 sixes and it is reliably reported he hit one ball out of the ground and into Trafalgar Square.

For Middlesex there were, strange to say, no such performances. His best score for the county was 79, made in 60 minutes with 11 fours and 2 fives against Oxford at Prince's

(on the site of Lennox Gardens) in 1876. Thornton's first-class career record was 6,928 runs, average 19.35, suggesting a lack of discrimination as to which balls to try and hit. Possibly an extremely superior sort of 'slogger'?

Thornton made his first-class debut aged sixteen for the 'Gentlemen of Kent' against MCC in 1866. The tyro scored 26 and 24 and contributed manfully to his side's win. He was subsequently a Cambridge Blue, played for Kent and MCC, and raised his own XI at the Scarborough festival. When he played here for the last time he had completed a first-class career of 31 years.

Thornton organised teams for Scarborough long after ceasing on-field participation. He was a successful businessman in the timber trade and an inveterate traveller. *Wisden* reported that when the First World War broke out he was in Berlin and 'was very nearly caught'. Whether he was batting at the time is not recorded.

Frederick John Titmus
RHB, RM, OB, 1949-1982

Born: 14 November 1932, St Pancras

Batting

M	I	NO	Runs	Av
642	931	171	17320	22.78
144	106	32	1020	13.78

50	100	ct/st
77	5	378
-	-	34

Bowling

Balls	Runs	Wkts	Av	5wI	10wM
139416	50223	2361	21.27	146	20
6940	3945	155	25.45	3	-

Best Performances
120* v. Sussex at Hove, 1961
41 v. Sussex at Lord's, 1973
9-52 v. Cambridge University at Fenner's, 1962
5-26 v. Derbyshire at Lord's, 1970

Fred Titmus enjoyed in some respects the most remarkable career of any Middlesex player. He made his debut in 1949 at 16 years 213 days, the youngest ever Middlesex cricketer. When he made his final appearance in 1982, he had established a record span of 33 seasons and at 50 years 276 days was the 4th oldest Middlesex player, and the oldest to appear for the county at Lord's.

An analysis of his career makes amazing reading. Pre-eminently his 2,361 wickets constitute a Middlesex record unlikely to be beaten, as also do his 158 wickets, average 14.63, in 1955. Titmus took 100 wickets for the county a record 11 times, while only John Thomas Hearne exceeds the 146 times he took 5 or more wickets in an innings. Titmus's four 1,000 runs/100 wickets 'doubles' has been beaten for Middlesex only by Francis Tarrant. Titmus' best innings bowling analysis was 9 for 52 against Cambridge University at Fenner's in 1962; two years later his 9 for 57 against Lancashire was, and still is, the best innings analysis at Lord's for any county since 1929. At Oxford in 1968, Titmus' figures of 6 for 5 in

13 overs were, statistically, the best innings figures ever for Middlesex. Against Somerset at Bath in 1955, innings figures of 8 for 44 and 7 for 51 combined for a match return of 15 for 95, the best for the county since the First World War. Titmus had an affinity with Somerset festivals. He made his debut at Bath in 1949 and achieved the figures just quoted there six years later. At Weston in 1966, he achieved his only hat-trick.

Titmus was a technically correct batsman with a free drive who may have made the grade had he never bowled a ball. Six times he exceeded 1,000 runs in a season with an impressive best of 1,579 runs, average 35.89, in 1961, one of his 'double' seasons. Against the 1965 South Africans Titmus added 227 with Clive Radley, a sixth-wicket record until 1994. As an all-rounder he is one of only 3 players to exceed 10,000 runs and 1,000 wickets for Middlesex. Not renowned for his fielding, Titmus' 378 catches nevertheless place

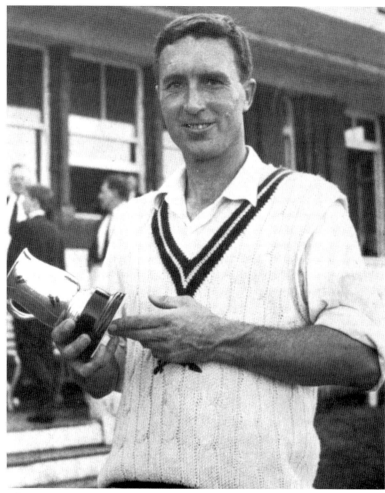

Titmus with a cup for winning the Charrington Single-Wicket Competition in 1966.
He beat B. Cowper of Australia in the final.

him 6th on the list; doubtless most were taken with the same quiet, almost invisible reliability with which he played all his cricket.

While making his 642 appearances for Middlesex, Titmus between times played 53 Tests for England between 1955 and 1975. His figures of 1,449 runs (av. 22.29), 153 wickets (32.22) and 35 catches in no way either over or underrate his value.

So effective a player was Titmus it seems a major pity that his other cricketing activities were so undistinguished. His spell as county captain, from 1965 until his resignation midway through 1968, was marked by the sort of negative thinking and ill-success for the team likely to destroy all spectator interest. In his spell as coach across the river at The Oval, Titmus made little impact and while he no doubt did his best as a Test selector, there was little sign that he really knew what the job was supposed to entail, or that he had a great deal to offer.

As a cricketer, however, there is no doubt whatsoever that Fred Titmus was one of the best of post-war all-rounders. Total first-class career figures of 21,588 runs (23.11), 473 catches and 2,830 wickets (22.37) cannot lie. They alone justified the award of the MBE.

Albert Edwin Trott
RHB, RMOB, RF, 1898-1910

Born: 6 February 1873, Abbotsford, Melbourne,
Australia
Died: 30 July 1914, Harlesden, Willesden

Batting

M	I	NO	Runs	Av
323	341	32	6253	20.23

50	100	ct/st		
25	6	253		

Bowling

Balls	Runs	Wkts	Av	5wI	10wM
42572	20332	946	21.49	71	23

Best Performances
164 v. Yorkshire at Lord's, 1899
10-42 v. Somerset at Taunton, 1900

'Alberto' was one of Middlesex cricket's most tragic figures, an exceptional all-rounder who for various reasons dissipated much of his talent and, finding little left in life, blew out his own brains with a pistol.

Trott played for Victoria and Australia but, excluded from the 1896 Australian touring party, worked his way to England, joined the Lord's staff and began his Middlesex qualification. He immmediately established himself as a brilliant natural bowler, who varied his pace from medium to fast and spun a vicious off-break in his huge right hand. Trott was also a powerful batsman who for MCC against the 1899 Australians hit M.A. Noble over the Lord's pavilion, a unique feat. Rumour had it that he spoiled his batting trying to repeat the blow, but he did in fact enjoy his best batting season in 1900 and as late as 1906 was scoring consistently. Another frequently repeated Trott legend is that by performing two hat-tricks in the second innings of his benefit match against Somerset in 1907, he ruined himself financially. In fact there was a poor third-day crowd, most of the money would have been taken on the first two days when the match took a more conventional route, so his third-day fireworks would have had virtually no financial effect whatsoever.

In his early Middlesex years, Trott was a superb player. In 1899 he took 150 wickets (av. 15.98) and the following season 154 wickets (19.85). He remains second to Titmus (158). In both these seasons he exceeded 1,000 runs and 200 wickets in all first-class matches, the first recording of this rare feat. Trott also exceeded 100 wickets in 1898, his debut season for the county, a feat matched only by Jim Smith in 1934. Against Somerset at Taunton in 1900, Trott became the first Middlesex bowler to take all ten. His 10 for 42 in 14.2 overs remained unbeaten until 1929. In the following game Trott achieved second innings figures of 8 for 47 against Gloucestershire at Clifton, match-decisive performances on the sometimes gruelling Western tour. On four other occasions Trott took 8 wickets in an innings, but the last was against Essex in 1901.

"A. E."

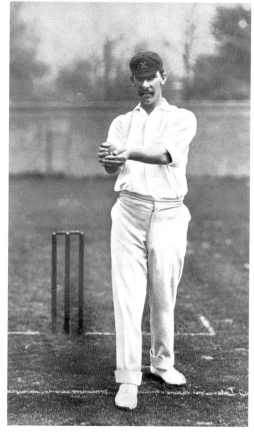

Trott enjoyed some triumphant matches. He took 10 or more wickets in a match 23 times for Middlesex, a record exceeded by J.T. Hearne alone. In 1899 he achieved the feat a record 7 times; the previous record was 5, by Trott in 1898. His best match figures were 15 for 187 against Sussex at Lord's in 1901: 8 for 115 followed by 7 for 72, and he dismissed every Sussex batsman at least once. More spectacular statistically were his efforts against Somerset at Lord's in 1899. He and Hearne bowled unchanged and following 4 for 18 with 7 for 13, Trott's match return was 11 for 31 in 15 overs. Unsurprisingly, Middlesex were innings victors.

Trott achieved two hat-tricks for Middlesex, both in the second innings of his benefit match against Somerset in 1907, and he was way over the hill. It was perhaps typical 'Alberto' that he reserved such bowling for

so important an occasion; far from ruining his benefit it made it unforgettable. In this match he also became the first Middlesex bowler to take 4 wickets with consecutive balls. Only Frank Tarrant subsequently equalled him.

Trott twice performed the 'match double' of 100 runs and 10 wickets, with scores of 123 and 35* and bowling figures of 6 for 132 and 6 for 68 against Sussex at Lord's in 1899, and 112 and bowling analyses of 8 for 54 and 3 for 84 in 1901 against Essex at Lord's. These first such feats for Middlesex in the Championship won both matches.

By received reckoning, Albert Trott played Test cricket for both Australia and England. He scored 228 runs (av. 38.00) and took 26 wickets (15.00). In all first-class cricket his record was 10,696 runs (19.48) and 1,674 wickets (21.09). But figures do not tell the full tale of this larger than life but tragic character.

Philip Clive Roderick Tufnell
RHB, SLA, 1986 to date

Born: 29 April 1966, Barnet, Herts.

Batting

M	I	NO	Runs	Av
239	265	93	1852	10.76
73	26	13	110	8.46

50	100	ct/st
I	-	78
-	-	13

Bowling

Balls	Runs	Wkts	Av	5wI	10wM
59516	23714	842	28.16	42	4
3643	2628	84	31.28	I	-

Best Performances
67* v. Worcestershire at Lord's, 1996
18 v. Warwickshire at Lord's, 1991
8-29 v. Glamorgan at Cardiff, 1993
5-28 v. Lancashire at Lord's, 1993

Phil Tufnell, one of the more interesting Middlessex personalities of recent years, established himself as a left-armed spinner always likely to produce the unexpected and to a degree he has fulfilled expectations.

Tufnell first came to notice as Edmonds' likely successor at Canterbury in 1987 when second innings figures of 6 for 60 on a slow pitch (figures which matched those of Kent's left arm maestro, Derek Underwood) nearly saw his county to an unexpected win in a dire season. In 1989, Tufnell exceeded 50 wickets for the first time and in 1990 he pushed his total to 74. The cost of 35.43 runs apiece seemed high but England's selectors were sufficiently impressed to include him in the 1990/91 Australian touring party, where he produced moderate figures, but immoderate behaviour.

For varying reasons Tufnell, who should have been at his peak in the mid-1990s, never established himself for England, though he had his moments. For Middlesex, however, he usually did pretty well, regularly exceeding 70 wickets in a season, with a best of 78, average 21.94, in 1996. There were some fine performances, among which were match figures of 11 for 228 in 72.4 overs against Hampshire at Lord's in 1991. Middlesex lost the match, but the dire support was hardly Tufnell's fault. A more positive result attended his best career figure, a superb 8 for 29 in 28 overs against Glamorgan at Cardiff in 1993. Middlesex won by 10 wickets despite double centuries from two Glamorgan batsmen. As Tufnell's results and reliability declined, his value also deteriorated, but there were shafts of light. Tufnell was no doubt delighted when he outbowled his England successor, Giles, at Edgbaston in 2001, ensuring a much-needed win in a table-topping clash. His match figures of 6 for 106, against Giles' 3 for 186 suggested he was still England material – a theory unfortunately not borne out by his subsequent performance in what was surely his final Test. In the Edgbaston game, Tufnell also sadly confirmed that he was a cricketer with problems; his treatment of a young autograph hunter, and the bad language which accompanied the rebuff were disgraceful and totally inexcusable.

George Frederick Vernon

RHB, RA underarm, 1878-1895

Born: 20 June 1856, Marylebone
Died: 10 August 1902, Elmina, Gold Coast (Ghana)

Batting

M	I	NO	Runs	Av
103	171	10	3048	18.93

50	100	ct/st
11	1	61

Bowling

Balls	Runs	Wkts	Av	5wI	10wM
-	-	-	-	-	-

Best Performances
106 v. Surrey at The Oval, 1880

George Vernon was an amateur batter, more rugged than polished but with a positive swing of the bat, a good field and a very occasional bowler of what may perhaps have been called 'slow cobs'. Unfortunately, no Middlesex skipper of his time would ever trust him to bowl a single ball.

As a specialist batsman, Vernon was not perhaps so regular a scorer as expected, especially since his only century was such a notable affair. On the first morning of the match with Surrey at The Oval in 1880 Vernon went in first with his skipper Isaac Walker and by lunch had scored 106 out of 136-2, an innings including 2 fours and 1 five in a single over from the left-armed pace bowler, Emmanuel Blamires. He was dismissed immediately after lunch and Middlesex totalled only 179, sufficient, however, to bring them an innings win. The next best score for Middlesex was 16, while no-one for Surrey exceeded 25. Vernon never again showed such form, though in the following sea-

son against Nottinghamshire, at Trent Bridge going in at number 8 he did hit 97 out of the 131 scored while he was at the wicket.

Vernon's main claim to cricket fame occured when he accepted an invitation from the Melbourne Cricket Club to take a team to Australia in the winter of 1887/88. Unfortunately, Shaw & Shrewsbury also took a team there and the result was financial disaster all round. The rival teams did get together for one Test match and won well. Vernon's only Test was for Ivo Bligh's team in 1882/83, when he achieved little. In all first-class cricket Vernon scored 7,070 runs, av. 19.10. Highest of his four centuries was 160 for MCC v. Oxford at Lord's in 1886. His runs came out of only 227 while he was at the wickets; he hit 22 fours but was dropped six times.

Vernon won 5 England caps for rugby football and twice won the Prince's annual cup for rackets. This true amateur sportsman died of malaria while visiting the Gold Coast.

Isaac Donnithorne Walker
RHB, RF underhand or slow lobs, 1862-1884

Born: 8 January 1844, Southgate
Died: 6 July 1898, Regent's Park, London

Batting

M	I	NO	Runs	Av
144	257	19	6065	25.48

50	100	ct/st		
35	4	138		

Bowling

Balls	Runs	Wkts	Av	5wI	10wM
7015	3151	152	20.73	8	1

Best Performances
145 v. Gloucestershire at Clifton, 1893
6-42 v. Nottinghamshire at Prince's, 1875

I.D. Walker was one of the seven bachelor brothers (the Seven Proud Walkers immortalised by W.A. Bettesworth in *The Walkers of Southgate* in 1900) who played for Middlesex between 1862 and 1884, a tall upstanding batsman with a fine drive, an excellent fielder and an underarm bowler, his repertoire ranging from slow, high, tossed lobs to quick and low. He also captained Middlesex between 1873 and 1884 and was on the committee until his death.

Isaac first played for the county in 1862 against the Surrey Club team at The Oval and hit a marvellous, second innings 102, adding 108 for the first wicket with his brother Russell. At 18 years and 217 days he is still beaten only by Denis Compton as the youngest batsman to score a century for Middlesex. Isaac remained a member of the side for more than twenty years and it is likely that he and his brothers exercised a considerable influence on county affairs. Isaac scored only three more centuries for Middlesex. Against Oxford at Prince's

ground in 1876 he scored 110, and repeated the dose with 128 for Middlesex against the same opposition at Lord's in 1881, but his best innings came in 1883. Now a veteran, he scored a dashing 145, with 2 sixes and 17 fours against Gloucestershire at Clifton, and added 324 with Alfred Lyttelton. It was at that time the best-ever stand in first-class cricket and remained the Middlesex second-wicket record until 1914.

I.D. Walker's bowling was generally underused. His best innings analysis was 6 for 42 against Nottinghamshire at Prince's in 1875 and as late as the Gloucestershire match in 1884, he had match winning figures of 10 for 72, but he bowled far less than his abilities warranted.

He played much for MCC and Gentlemen's sides and scored 11,400 runs (av. 24.51) and took 218 wickets and 248 catches in all first-class cricket. Sadly he had no part in the 'new-fangled' Test cricket. How, one wonders, would Australia have taken him?

117

Russell Donnithorne Walker

RHB, RA slow, 1862-1877

Born: 13 February 1842, Southgate
Died: 29 March 1922, Regent's Park, London

Batting

M	I	NO	Runs	Av
45	78	2	1678	22.07
50	100	ct/st		
4	1	36		

Bowling

Balls	Runs	Wkts	Av	5wI	10wM
5352	2492	142	17.54	9	1

Best Performances
104 v. Surrey at The Oval, 1876
6-76 v. Sussex at Hove, 1864

R.D. Walker, of the famous and proud Southgate brotherhood was a right-handed batsman who could play a steady game or hit hard according to the situation. He was also reported to be a 'curly' slow round-arm bowler and a fine field anywhere. Shorter and stockier than his taller, slimmer brothers, Russie Walker was also unusual in that he left the family home early in adult life to live at The Albany, Piccadilly.

Walker's best score for Middlesex, and his only century, was 104 against Surrey at The Oval in 1876. He went in with the score at 9 for 1 in the second innings and stayed while 254 runs were added before being seventh out. Set 246 to win Surrey seemed to be struggling but good stands for the later wickets put them in the game but finally matters ended in a tie.

Walker had several fine performances as a bowler, the best being against Sussex at Hove in 1864, when he followed first innings figures of 5 for 54 with 6 for 76, fine bowling in a losing cause as Middlesex went down by three wickets. Another excellent bowling performance came in 1865 against the 'crack' Surrey team at The Oval. Russie Walker came on to take the last 5 Surrey wickets for 13 runs to send the South London rivals crashing to defeat. Walker's best bowling season came in 1866. He took 39 wickets at 14.80. Against Nottinghamshire at Trent Bridge he had match figures of 8 for 73 (he and Tom Hearne bowled unchanged) and scored 90 in his only innings. He also held three catches and can be said to have played a huge part in the innings victory. Walker took 5 wickets in an innings three more times in what was a very fine season. In 1867 against Nottinghamshire at Islington, he had innings figures of 6 for 91. Against Yorkshire at Princes in 1873, Walker had match figures of 7 for 18 as the visitors were quite overplayed.

Walker won an Oxford Blue 1861 to 1865; in his career he scored nearly 4,000 runs and took 334 wickets in important cricket. He was a fine player indeed.

Vyell Edward Walker
RHB, RA slow underhand, 1859-1877

Born: 20 April 1837, Southgate
Died: 3 January 1906, Arnos Grove

Batting

M	I	NO	Runs	Av
52	82	8	1310	17.70

50	100	ct/st
7	-	16

Bowling

Balls	Runs	Wkts	Av	5wl	10wM
-	-	130	-	13	3

Best Performances
87* v. Surrey at The Oval, 1865
10-104 v. Lancashire at Old Trafford, 1865

Edward Walker, at his peak, was arguably the best of the seven Southgate brothers, an orthodox batsman with special certainty on the leg side and a bowler of slow flighted lobs. He also captained the side between 1864 and 1872.

The fifth of the brothers reached his all-round peak at a comparatively early age, being only twenty-two when he scored 20* and 108, and had bowling figures of 10 for 74 and 4 for 17 for England v. Surrey at The Oval in 1859. These remained his best batting and bowling returns. For Middlesex, he never reached three figures and bowled somewhat less than one would expect but had some fine performances, none more so than when he took all 10 wickets in the innings, for 104, against Lancashire at Old Trafford in 1865. It was a fine captain's effort, albeit in a losing cause. The previous season he had achieved figures of 9 for 62 (innings) and 14 for 103 (match) to overwhelm Sussex at the Islington Cattle Market ground.

In important matches during his career V.E. Walker scored more than 3,300 runs, took 350 wickets and 200 catches, but it cannot be said that he really fulfilled his early promise and into his thirties he practically gave up bowling.

As a batsman, his finest day for Middlesex came against Surrey at Islington in 1866. He and Tom Hearne achieved a record sixth-wicket stand for the county of 161, and Walker's share was 79, run out. This was his best score for Middlesex until 1867 when he scored 87* against Surrey at The Oval, the highest score of the match, which saved Middlesex from almost certain defeat.

In 1891, V.E. Walker was president of MCC and from 1899 until his death in 1906 he held the same position with Middlesex. V.E. Walker's services to Middlesex cricket are incontrovertible, his captaincy of the county was totally unselfish, yet somehow he failed to really fulfil his promise and his cricketing achievements were strangely disappointing.

Born: 2 October 1873, Port-of-Spain, Trinidad

Died: 30 January 1963, West Lavington, Sussex

Batting

M	I	NO	Runs	Av
345	571	50	19507	37.44
50	100	ct/st		
94	46	123		

Bowling

Balls	Runs	Wkts	Av	5wI	10wM
337	198	4	49.50	-	-

Best Performances

197* v. Somerset at Lord's, 1901

'Plum' Warner was, for some sixty years, one of the best-known figures in world cricket, as well as the ultimate father-figure of the Middlesex club, and Lord's ground.

Born into an old Trinidadian settler family, his father being Attorney-General of the island (and incidentally born before the battle of Trafalgar), Warner learned his cricket at home but the bug really bit when he went to Rugby school aged thirteen. As a batsman, Warner was usually of the steady school but despite a lack of physical power he had a range of attacking strokes, including a hard drive and a delicate late cut, and on occasions was known to create surprise at the way he forced the pace.

Warner captained the county for nine seasons from 1908 to 1920 and marked his last season with a remarkable first place. They won their last 9 matches off the reel yet still required an unlikely last day victory to secure the title. The final, vital win, was satisfyingly over local rivals Surrey. Had Surrey won that last match (perfectly possible until late on) they would have been runners-up and Lancashire champions, with Middlesex down to third place. No wonder Warner was carried from the pitch in triumph and into happy retirement.

Perhaps Warner's figures place him a little below the greatest, but he has 14th place as a Middlesex run-scorer and was first to reach 10,000 runs for the county, while he is 8th in number of centuries. Surprisingly, Warner never scored a double century for the county; his best score for Middlesex was an unbeaten 197 against Somerset at Lord's in 1901, a splendid effort occupying four and a half hours, and he carried his bat through an innings total of 400. It is surely a tribute to Warner's soundness that no Middlesex player

Sir Pelham Warner, elder statesman of Middlesex cricket.

has beaten the 7 times he carried his bat. His aggressive abilities were shown when against Surrey at The Oval in 1907 he reached 115* on the first morning. In a period of fewer championship matches, Warner exceeded 1,000 runs in a season on ten occasions.

Against Nottinghamshire at Trent Bridge in 1904, Warner and James Douglas added 306 runs together. This was to remain the Middlesex first-wicket record until 1947. He also added 232 with Douglas when scoring his pre-lunch century mentioned above. This is still the best for the Middlesex first wicket against Surrey. He added 248 with L.J. Moon against Gloucestershire at Lord's in 1903, the county record first wicket at the time, and as late as 1920 against Sussex at Lord's, Warner put on 241 with Harry Lee.

Warner played in 15 Tests and was skipper on 10 occasions, but 622 runs (av. 23.92) was unremarkable. In all first-class cricket Warner scored 29,028 runs (36.28); the best of his 60 centuries was 244 for The Rest against the 1911 county champions, Warwickshire.

For many years Warner was a Test selector, and in 1932/33 he managed the 'bodyline' tour but seemed to stand idly by when matters became heated. In 1937, however, he was knighted for his services to the game and in 1950 was MCC president. He founded *The Cricketer* magazine in 1921 and maintained his connections until his death – albeit mainly inactive in later years. He had a reputation as a cricket writer, and produced, or was closely connected with more than 20 books. Overall, cricket is in his debt.

John James Warr

RHB, RFM, 1949-1960

Born: 16 July 1927, Ealing

Batting

M	I	NO	Runs	Av
260	344	90	2744	10.80
50	100	ct/st		
1	-	91		

Bowling

Balls	Runs	Wkts	Av	5wI	10wM
36884	14592	703	20.75	24	3

Best Performances

51 v. Worcestershire at Worcester, 1955
9-65 v. Kent at Lord's, 1956

Tall with long arms, John Warr was an enthusiastic fast-medium bowler with the furious action of someone much quicker. He showed great promise at Cambridge, where he won a Blue 4 times and was a surprise choice for the 1950/51 MCC tour of Australia and although not quite the Test success as might have been hoped, as well as having to be taught to field properly, he did his bit in state games and was a popular team member.

For Middlesex, Warr was capped in 1949 and after leaving Cambridge played regularly, and effectively until 1960. In his last three seasons, he led the county and in a difficult period he left the team better than he found it.

Warr twice exceeded 100 wickets in a season for the county, his best being 108, average 16.16, in the batsman's summer of 1959. Undoubtedly this was his peak, but he also did well in 1956, the other season with a three-figure return. Against Kent at Lord's in 1956, he followed a first innings analysis of 5 for 27, with his best-ever 9 for 65 in 15.2 overs. Earlier in the season, his hostility in helpful conditions had seen him skittle Nottinghamshire with 8 for 26 and these performances remained the best of his career. 1956 also saw Warr's only hat-trick, at Loughborough against Leics.

Warr's batting was often sub-standard, but he occasionally proved useful. In his first-class career as a whole he scored 3,838 runs (av. 11.45) and took 956 wickets (av. 22.79). His Test 'career', which gave him one expensive wicket, left him 'weary, laboured and sore distressed.'

After retirement Warr became an administrator, and in 1987/88 was MCC president. He also became a writer, in which capacity it was sometimes difficult to spot the line between fact and fantasy, but he always entertained the reader. Warr was similarly entertaining as an after-dinner speaker and raconteur, and season-ticket holder at Bill Edrich's numerous weddings.

Alexander Josiah Webbe
RHB, RFM, WKT, 1875-1900

Born: 16 January 1855, Bethnal Green, London
Died: 19 February 1941, Abinger Hammer, Surrey

Batting

M	I	NO	Runs	Av
247	430	44	9405	24.33
50	**100**	**ct/st**		
39	7	149/6		

Bowling

Balls	Runs	Wkts	Av	5wI	10wM
5551	1989	68	29.25	2	-

Best Performances
243* v. Yorkshire at Huddersfield, 1887
5-23 v. Kent at Lord's, 1887

'Webbie' had a most unprepossessing stance at the wicket, crouching with legs bent and wide apart but he was sound in defence and had a good drive either side of the wicket. Webbe gained a towering reputation at Harrow and when he skippered Oxford for two seasons, graduation to the leadership of Middlesex was then a matter of course and he led them with good judgement, albeit with some reputation as a martinet, for 14 seasons.

Webbe began on a high note, carrying his bat for the first of 7 times, for 97* in his second match, against Nottinghamshire at Prince's in 1875, and his first hundred came against the same opposition in 1877. Webbe's best score came against Yorkshire at Huddersfield in 1887 – a stupendous 243*, at the time the record score for Middlesex, and still the best against Yorkshire. Webbe batted 370 minutes and hit 41 fours; carrying his bat out of 527 is both a record individual and total score for such a feat for Middlesex. In his previous match against Kent at Canterbury, Webbe had carried his bat for 192 out of 412, and earlier in the season he had batted throughout a total of 119 against Oxford for 63*. Three times in four matches is a record. Against Kent at Gravesend in 1886, Webbe added 205 for the first wicket with Andrew Stoddart. It was a short-lived record but set a benchmark for their successors.

Webbe was a useful quickish bowler whose occasional successful forays suggested underuse. Against Kent at Lord's in 1887, his second innings figures of 5 for 23 nipped in the bud a Kent recovery to ensure victory for his side.

Webbe's full first-class record was 14,465 runs (av. 24.81), 109 wickets (25.21), 227 catches and 10 stumpings. Clearly on his day he was a class player yet surprisingly played only one, unsuccessful, Test match.

From 1923 to 1936 Webbe was Middlesex president; he also served on the committee for some years. His brother H.R. Webbe showed early promise for Middlesex but died young.

Paul Nicholas Weekes

LHB, OB, 1990 to date

Born: 8 July 1969, Hackney, London

Batting

M	I	NO	Runs	Av
175	270	36	7995	34.16
251	217	35	4747	26.08

50	100	ct/st
38	15	166
22	3	106

Bowling

Balls	Runs	Wkts	Av	5wI	10wM
18883	9004	222	40.55	4	-
9570	7572	273	27.73	13	-

Best Performances

171* v. Somerset at Uxbridge, 1996
143* v. Cornwall at St Austell, 1995
8-39 v. Glamorgan at Lord's, 1996
4-17 v. Kent at Lord's, 2001

Paul Weekes has been, always worthy of his corn, yet there is the feeling that something more than county cricket could have beckoned.

An East Ender, Weekes' county debut against Somerset at Uxbridge in 1990 could have been more propitious. He fell foul of an ultimately unsuccessful bid for full batting points by ex-Middlesex player Graham Rose who scored 57 in 38 balls, 26 of the runs coming in one over from the unfortunate Weekes. Overall, he bowled well in unsympathetic conditions and his all round promise was confirmed later in the season against Sussex. Going in at number 8, he scored 51 and actually dominated a 96-run stand with Desmond Haynes.

Weekes continued to promise as a batsman but lack of opportunity fatally prevented his development as an off spinner. A maiden century came against Somerset at Lord's in 1994 – his 117 was part of a 264 seventh-wicket stand with John Carr – but he was still seemingly underused and Weekes would have been excused feelings of frustration.

Weekes finally emerged as a genuine batting force in 1996 for the first and so far only time exceeding 1,000 runs for the county. His 1,218 runs (average 36.90) included 4 centuries and a career best 171 not out against Somerset at Uxbridge. His bowling was again generally disappointing but he enjoyed one marvellous spell against Glamorgan at Lord's. In the second innings he took 8 for 30 in 20 overs, finishing with 5 for 7 in his last 34 balls. He then hit 40 in 30 minutes to win the match.

Weekes' all round form in subsequent seasons has been somewhat mixed but 40 wickets, average 29.95, in 2001 suggested that although the latent bowling talent had never been allowed to flower some ability remained, while a batting average of over 50 in the successful promotion campaign of 2002 certainly stressed his value.

Weekes has of course been a valuable member of the limited-overs outfit, and his all-round efforts certainly helped cement his position as a vital cog in the first-team squad. Although early performances suggested more, talent denied opportunity stands for little.

Cyril Mowbray Wells
RHB, LB, 1895-1909

Born: 21 March 1871, St Pancras, London
Died: 22 August 1963, St John's Wood

Batting

M	I	NO	Runs	Av
113	166	24	3383	23.82

50	100	ct/st		
13	4	83		

Bowling

Balls	Runs	Wkts	Av	5wI	10wM
15457	7183	350	20.52	21	2

Best Performances
244 v. Nottinghamshire at Trent Bridge, 1899
8-35 v. Yorkshire at Headingley, 1900

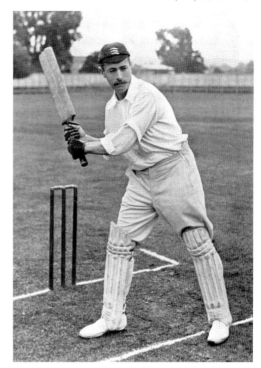

Cyril Mowbray Wells was a gifted all-rounder whose profession as a schoolmaster at Eton prevented his ever being able to play regularly for the county but who maintained form remarkably well. Wells was a stroke-playing batsman, a versatile slow bowler who usually turned from leg but had many variations, and an excellent close field.

Wells won his Blue at Cambridge in three seasons and also played a handful of games for Surrey before throwing in his lot with Middlesex. Wells scored the first of his four county centuries against Somerset at Taunton in 1898. He and F.H.E. Cunliffe added 110 for the eighth wicket in 70 minutes and Wells himself was batting only 100 minutes for his 101. The following season he played his finest ever innings, a dashing 244 in 345 minutes against Nottinghamshire at Trent Bridge. It was a triumphant match for Wells, who also took 9 wickets for 111 and played a great part in an innings victory. When scoring 105 against Essex in Leyton in 1902 Wells added 208 for the fifth wicket with James Douglas

and took 9 wickets in this match also. Wells' other century came in 1901, 124* against Somerset at Taunton. It followed a first innings 69 and he was top scorer in both innings. He also took 5 first innings wickets and bowled 39.4 overs. It was no fault of Wells' that a win could not be forced.

Wells twice took 8 wickets in an innings, the best being 8 for 35 against Yorkshire at Headingley in 1900, when he had match figures of 13 for 68 yet finished on the losing side, but against Nottinghamshire at Trent Bridge in 1895 second innings figures of 8 for 38 gave a match analysis of 12 for 71, and helped materially toward an 8-wicket victory. Such performances as these, and first-class career figures of 4,229 runs (22.02) and 465 wickets (19.86), suggest that he was a fine player whose chosen profession perhaps prevented his playing Test cricket. He was a Rugby Blue at Cambridge and played twice for England; despite his playing county cricket only in his holidays he could well have been close to becoming a double international.

John Edward West
RHB, RM, WKT, 1885-1896

Born: 11 November 1861, Stepney, London
Died: 14 March 1920, Bow, E. London

Batting

M	I	NO	Runs	Av
76	127	13	1406	12.33
50	100	ct/st		
2	-	73/24		

Bowling

Balls	Runs	Wkts	Av	5wI	10wM
4749	2052	82	25.02	4	-

Best Performances
83 v. Gloucestershire at Lord's, 1888
6-31 v. Kent at Lord's, 1886

East Ender John West was a genuine 'bits 'n pieces' player a century before such a term was generally adopted. He batted, bowled, kept wicket, fielded anywhere, whatever was required of him.

West's county debut, against Surrey at The Oval in 1885 was fairly undistinguished. He took a couple of wickets, but bagged a 'pair'. Such form could mean only one thing – promotion. In the next game, against Yorkshire at Lord's he opened with A.J. Webbe, defying a strong attack well to score 42. In the second innings of the following game, the Surrey return at Lord's, West proved his worth with second innings figures of 5 for 20. He and James Robertson skittled Surrey for 61 but Middlesex still lost. Later that season West had innings figures of 5 for 51 against Yorkshire, and an aggressive 67 against Gloucestershire at Clifton confirmed his all round promise.

In 1886, his bowling ability was certainly proved. In the season's first game against Kent at Lord's he ripped through the visitors' batting with first innings figures of 6 for 31 to set up an easy win. These figures were to remain his best but he bowled well throughout the season, topping the averages with 32 wickets at 17.96, though his batting went to pieces. This was partially recovered in 1888 whe he scored a fine 83 against Gloucestershire – and was promptly dropped!

West's bowling form then dipped alarmingly and his county career may have ended prematurely had he not, in 1889, solved a problem by taking over as wicketkeeper. 21 dismissals in 8 matches was a pretty satisfactory return, especially for a comparative novice, while his 9 stumpings suggested that he was a 'proper' wicketkeeper. West maintained his form in 1890 and against Gloucestershire at Lord's he had 5 stumpings in the match – a feat that remains unbeaten to this day, but is sadly unpublicised. Equally sadly, after two seasons as regular 'keeper, West found his appearances less frequent. He never bowled, did not always keep wicket and his batting was not good enough for him to be a specialist. West gave years of unstinting service on the Lord's staff.

Neil FitzGerald Williams
RHB, RFM, 1982-1994

Born: 12 July 1962, Hopewell, St Vincent

Batting

M	I	NO	Runs	Av
193	209	45	3027	18.45
193	93	31	755	12.17

50	100	ct/st
9	-	46
-	-	41

Bowling

Balls	Runs	Wkts	Av	5wI	10wM
27631	14675	479	30.63	12	1
8751	6087	205	29.69	-	-

Best Performances
77 v. Warwickshire at Edgbaston, 1991
43 v. Somerset at Lord's, 1988
8-75 v. Gloucestershire at Lord's, 1992
4-36 v. Derbyshire at Derby, 1983

The rather exotically named Neil FitzGerald Williams was a lively seam bowler who was most surprisingly selected for England against India in 1990, and even more surprisingly then dropped for ever, yet another example of the legendary foresight and sensitivity of the England selectors.

Williams first sprung to the fore in 1983 when consistent work, often without other seam support, brought 63 wickets (av. 26.33). Williams then 'trod water' for some seasons, and missed most of 1986 through injury. Back problems recurred in 1988, though when he played he was accurate and lively. Williams came back strongly in 1990 when some good performances included his best innings analysis of 7 for 61 in 22 overs against Kent at Lord's, when his pace and accuracy proved too much for most of the visitors, and he earned his sole Test call.

Williams really reached his peak as a consistent performer in 1990. For the next four seasons his performances were largely mediocre, and affected by fitness problems, but spells when he did little were interspersed with the occasional good figures. Against Gloucestershire at Lord's in 1992 for instance, he produced career best innings figures of 8 for 75 'seaming the ball around at a sharp pace' according to *Wisden*, but there were too few good performances such as these and after 1994 he left and joined Hampshire where sadly he really achieved little.

As a batsman, Williams sometimes promised without ever really delivering. His best contribution with the bat was his furious 77 from 67 deliveries, with 4 sixes all off Munton, against Warwickshire at Edgbaston in 1991. His overall record was useful, he had a good eye, but could perhaps have performed better with more application.

127

John Albert Young

RHB, SLA, 1933-1956

Born: 14 October 1912, Paddington, London
Died: 5 February 1993, St John's Wood

Batting

M	I	NO	Runs	Av
292	343	95	2124	8.56
50	100	ct/st		
1	-	125		

Bowling

Balls	Runs	Wkts	Av	5wI	10wM
68452	22709	1182	19.21	70	14

Best Performances

62 v. Yorkshire at Sheffield, 1949
8-31 v. Yorkshire at Lord's, 1946

Jack Young's career was interrupted badly by the Second World War but after the resumption of the county game he still enjoyed an eleven-year span. At his peak he was one of the finest left-armed spinners to represent the county.

Smallish and dark, and reputedly with a penchant for 'rhyming slang', Jack Young had a springy, slightly jerky run up but the action was well oiled, length and direction as if set by a metronome and the flight and spin just enough to tease, torment and, very often, dismiss.

Young's first full season was 1946, when he took 101 wickets, the first of seven occasions when 100-plus wickets were taken, a figure exceeded only by J.T. Hearne and Titmus, and both played far longer. His best wicket return was 142, av. 21.01 in 1952, a season when he took his benefit but also suffered

knee injuries and a broken finger yet missed only one match, in a remarkable tribute to his persistence and spirit.

Young established himself in May 1946 with figures of 5 for 11 against Somerset but more satisfaction must have been felt with a second innings return of 8 for 31 against Yorkshire at Lord's in June. These remained his best-ever figures, but his match return of 12 for 72 was beaten two years later with 14 for 97 against Surrey at The Oval. He had figures of 7 for 50 and 7 for 47; in the previous game, at Northampton, he had 5 for 65 and 7 for 25. Against Northants in 1946, Jack Young achieved a 'hat-trick' during a spell of 5 for 8 in 3 overs; he repeated the '3-in-3' feat against Lancashire at Lord's in 1951. Of the county's comparatively few left armers, Young took the most wickets, and at a very small cost.

Jack Young's first-class record saw him score 2,485 tail-end runs at 8.93, but his total of 1,361 wickets, average 19.68, was very fine indeed given his interrupted career. For an England XI against The Commonwealth at Hastings in 1951 he had an innings analysis of 9 for 55, and this remained his best. His 17 wickets in 8 Tests are unrepresentative of the abilities of this dogged and quick-witted Londoner.